ENCOUNTERS OF A DIPLOMATIC KIND

ENCOUNTERS OF
A DIPLOMATIC KIND

by

RICHARD G. TALLBOYS

Richard G Tallboys (signature)

"Nanterre" March 2012 (handwritten)

Margaret Tallboys. (signature)

The Memoir Club

© Richard G. Tallboys 2009

First published in 2009 by
The Memoir Club
Arya House
Langley Park
Durham
DH7 9XE
Tel: 0191 373 5600

British Library Cataloguing in
Publication Data.
A catalogue record for this book
is available from the
British Library

ISBN: 978-1-84104-207-7

Typeset by TW Typesetting, Plymouth, Devon
Printed by Good News Press, Ongar, Essex CM5 9RX

I dedicate Encounters of A Diplomatic Kind *to my wife Margaret, who once said she was 'prepared to go anywhere at any time'. She hadn't bargained for it involving living in eleven countries, or for the fact that some of the countries would prove to be distinctly uncomfortable for diplomats and their wives. Margaret proved to be the ultimate diplomatic wife, one who could make friends across all cultural divides while putting up with difficult and sometimes dangerous living conditions. As for so many diplomatic wives, Margaret received no official recognition whatever for the contribution she made to my work over the twenty-six years of our peripatetic life. On the other hand she has no hesitation in saying that much of the experience was 'fun', not least for the many meetings with the 'rich and famous', experiences that at times led me to say that 'I stay in the Diplomatic Service to keep my wife amused'. Without Margaret none of it would have happened.*

Contents

List of Illustrations

Acknowledgements

I take the opportunity to acknowledge the support I received from the people who worked with me, not only in the overseas posts but also during my times in the Foreign & Commonwealth Office in London and in the Department of Trade in Canberra.

Much of any success I may have had was made possible by the support I received in the earlier years from Australian Assistant Trade Commissioners Ray Anderson in Singapore and Peter Dawson in Jakarta. Throughout my twenty years as a member of HM Diplomatic Service I had a long succession of excellent people to support me, and that includes many of the locally-engaged staff. Their names and faces all come readily to mind but the list is long and I would not wish to mention by name only some and not all. Many of them were fortunate in also having wives who accepted the complications to family life that arise in a diplomatic career, while giving support to my own wife when occasion arose. Suffice it to say that on careful reflection I cannot recall a single member of HM Diplomatic Service who worked with me once whom I would not have been happy to have arrive 'in post' to work with me again.

Preface

There seems little doubt that I have had an unusually varied career path, with a life filled with perhaps more interesting experiences than most people manage to squeeze in. Starting my working life at sea and then going on to a series of different careers that neither my parents, nor my teachers, nor my wife could have foreseen, has provided a long list of anecdotes to tell.

So I decided I should write a 'primer', producing for that purpose a collection of anecdotes from those stages of my life that involved representing two countries in the world of diplomacy. It would however perhaps be helpful to give readers some idea of what I got up to before I became a an Australian Government Trade Commissioner and then later a member of Her Majesty's Diplomatic Service. The two 'diplomatic' activities provided twenty-six years of what were certainly interesting employment, employment that fitted in well with what I did before and what I did afterwards. Experiences in each of my earlier careers turned out to be valuable in the later ones, an extreme example being perhaps when a major British company was saved a lot of money and a lot of trouble because the British Ambassador at Hanoi at the time just happened to be a chartered accountant with a law degree and a maritime background.

Applying to become an Australian Trade Commissioner was a logical career move that worked very satisfactorily for six years – and might have continued for a lot longer. On the other hand, the opportunity to apply to become a 'Late Entrant in the Administrative Grades of Her Majesty's Diplomatic Service' came about as one of several quirks of fate that have set my life off in unexpected ways. I may of course never get around to writing 'the rest of the story'. So I am going to start by providing in this Preface some brief details of my early years.

I was fortunate in my parents. I was fortunate in having a 'good war', with excellent foster parents while I was an evacuee for the first two years of World War 2. I was fortunate in the schools that I went to. I was fortunate in the shipping company with which I went to sea when I was sixteen. I was fortunate in the various employments I had. I was exceptionally fortunate in meeting Margaret.

The first war-time foster parents were an elderly couple in Suffolk; the second foster parents were a coal miner and his wife at a village in Warwickshire. They were all great people and in both cases lived close to some marvellous English countryside. I was then moved to Cornwall for a year at a very good primary school, St Paul's, in Truro, where I was able to live with my father who had himself been evacuated to Cornwall along with the school at which he taught in the East End of London.

My parents decided in 1942 that the bombing raids on London had declined sufficiently for it to be safe for me to return home to 'Bomb Alley' where my mother had remained, serving as an Air Raid Warden. I arrived home in time for the first night of the V1 'doodle-bugs'. My bedroom faced east, so standing at my window I had a first class view of what for an eleven-year old was the exciting spectacle of the noisy machines flying over the house belching flames from their jet engines; without me at the time having the faintest idea as to what they were or just how dangerous they could be.

My parents' purpose in bringing me home, not realising that bombing was in fact not all over, was so that having passed the 'Eleven-Plus' I could attend Palmers Endowed School for Boys, some 250 yards or so from our house gate. After my mother, two uncles and my two brothers, I was the sixth member of the family to go to the school. Palmers was not a 'public school' in the classification of Eton, Harrow etcetera, but the then headmaster, the Reverend 'Bunny' Abbott, had such a high reputation that he had been made an honorary member of the public schools' Headmasters Association.

My father's words and his choice of reading material were, along with good experiences of the school Army Cadet Force and the Boy Scouts, all part of the background that played a major part in forming my views of the world throughout my life. In the years before the war my father read to me from Kipling's *Jungle Books* and the *Just So Stories*. He encouraged me to read all the usual boys' books by authors such as G. A. Henty and his ilk, and books such as Southey's *Life of Nelson*. My father quoted often from Polonius's precepts to Laertes, from the homilies of Mr Micawber, and from Gilbert and Sullivan.

Seeing myself as becoming a latter day Nelson I had the early idea of becoming a midshipman in the Royal Navy. Fortunately, as it turned out, I did not do well enough to gain a scholarship to the Royal Naval College, Dartmouth. The next best thing seemed to me to be to go to sea in merchant ships. My parents were not enthusiastic about the idea of a seafaring career. Their minds were tuned more to the idea of me being an accountant or an actuary; but being good parents they ruled that I could go to sea providing I first obtained Matriculation for the University of London. At that point the excellent quality of the tuition at Palmers School played a deciding part. To some dismay on the part of my parents, and surprise on the part of my teachers, I obtained Matriculation Exemption at the age of fifteen. The dismay was I suspect because my parents were hoping the romantic idea of seafaring would wear off, and the surprise of the school was because I had, I regret, come to be seen as something of a 'slacker' – one who should 'try harder'.

Looking back I have come to wonder whether I really did want to go to sea or whether I just wanted to get away from school. Whatever the motivation I would have happily sailed off in any old tramp steamer or oil tanker that would take me. Fortunately none of them could take me until I had reached my sixteenth birthday. At a critical moment I was saved by an early quirk of fate that resulted in me going to sea with one of the finest British shipping companies: a company whose ships traded to Australia and New Zealand rather than to less salubrious parts of the world. Four years as a deck-officer apprentice in Port Line was a great way to spend my youth. In addition to a series of sea-faring adventures the years provided me with a lasting interest in ships and their cargoes.

The next quirk of fate was the circumstance of how I met Margaret. I was put ashore in Hobart to have my appendix removed. I required a week's convalescence before I could fly to Brisbane to rejoin my ship; so Margaret's father, who was the local agent for Port Line, told Margaret that she would have to look after me. Five years later, after seeing each other only intermittently as I continued at sea and Margaret did the young Australian 'thing' of travelling about Europe, we married.

Lesser quirks of fate led to my discovering that I could study accountancy by correspondence course while I earned a very good income as a Third Officer and later Second Officer of merchant ships on the Australian coast. Having obtained my first accountancy qualification I 'swallowed the anchor' – more or less – and so on and so forth until the most extraordinary of all the quirks of fate happened when it came to my notice that Her Majesty's Diplomatic Service had become interested in recruiting a few 'late entrants' with good university degrees and 'a commercial background'. By that time I had already moved on from eight years at sea, to eight years in the accountancy profession and to six years representing Australia as a Trade Commissioner in 'commercial diplomacy'. I had a handful of professional qualifications and had worked my way through a Bachelor of Commerce degree as a part-time student at the University of Tasmania.

I hope to be able in the not too distant future to tell my personal 'sea stories': including a blizzard off Cape Cod and a 93-day voyage on a very small vessel without radar, radio or refrigerator. There are also a few tales to tell of adventures in the accounting profession in Tasmania, especially of giving evidence as an expert witness in criminal trials. It was the lessons of four and a half days in the witness box for the defence in one trial, and half a day for the prosecution in another, that set me off on the road to my Bachelor of Laws at London University. At the other end of my working life there was also a very interesting period of five years of international work that required just as much diplomatic skill as I had ever needed. But those stories will have to wait. In this memoir I have set out to restrict my stories to some of the experiences from my twenty years as a member of Her Majesty's Diplomatic Service introduced by some mention of my time representing Australia as a Trade Commissioner in Africa and Asia.

All being well I shall in the near future get around to writing the 'The Rest of the Story'. In the meantime, in the words of Lord Tolloller in *Iolanthe*: 'And now to the business of the day.'

Richard G. Tallboys
September 2009

CHAPTER 1

A prelude in 'trade'

M Y INTEREST HAS ALWAYS TENDED towards the international trade side of diplomacy. My years at sea introduced me to the 'romance' of Masefield's 'butting through the Channel in the mad March days, . . . and cheap tin trays'. So taking up the opportunity in 1962 to become an Australian Government Trade Commissioner seemed a logical step to take. Six years representing Australia in 'trade' was most worthwhile and provided me with a great deal of worthwhile experience that came in useful when I moved on to 'straight' diplomacy and represented the United Kingdom as a member of Her Majesty's Diplomatic Service.

The two years 1962 to 1964 in Africa, including a spell as Acting Trade Commissioner for East Africa based in Nairobi, gave me an insight into African issues that I had certainly not gained from my early ship visits to Cape Town and Durban in the 1940s. The time in Kenya provided some understanding of tribal conflicts that still apply at the heart of violent problems throughout Africa south of the Sahara. If there is one thing that can certainly be blamed on Europeans it is the way in which politicians sat in European capitals dividing up the continent by drawing lines on maps without any regard to or understanding of the tribal divisions within the territories they were considering. The time in Johannesburg provided some insight into the stupidities of apartheid, while visits to Swaziland, Mozambique and Mauritius helped me to understand the wide divergencies of cultures in the region and the varying nature of colonial legacies.

The years as Australian Trade Commissioner in Singapore 1964–66 and in Jakarta 1966–67 were however particularly valuable and aroused in me a fascination with Asia and Asian business that added to my early brief seafaring visits to Sourbaya in 1952 and to Singapore and Manila in 1955.

Arriving in Singapore in 1964 as Assistant Trade Commissioner I was after a few months moved up to be Trade Commissioner for a territory that in addition to Singapore itself included Sarawak, Sabah and Brunei. I had opportunity to visit and get to know all three of the subsidiary territories before the separation of Singapore from Malaysia cut them out of my area

1

of responsibility for promoting Australian exports. There was plenty to keep me occupied in newly independent Singapore.

Singapore now talks in terms of 10 August 1965 as the day the island state 'gained' independence. In reality Singaporeans had independence thrust upon them by a decision made solely by the wise statesman Tungku Abdul Rahman who had come to realise that the addition of Singapore to Malaysia in 1963 had presented him with a problematic large increase in the minority Chinese population of his country. The Tungku in effect threw Singapore out of Malaysia without so much as telling Lee Kwan Yew in advance. The headline across the front page of the Singapore *Straits Times* that day simply said 'SINGAPORE IS OUT'. Of some additional embarrassment perhaps is that an item further down the front page read: 'Prime Minister Lee Kwan Yew, with tears in his eyes, urged the people of Singapore to remain calm.' By chance I have in my possession a facsimile of that front page. The matter is a very sensitive one for Singapore, so sensitive that when a friend of ours was commissioned a few years ago to write a history of the *Straits Times* newspaper, she was not made aware of that particular front page. I have throughout the years been a great admirer of Lee Kwan Yew and the way Singapore has been managed since 1965. As early as my naval visit to Singapore in 1955 I wrote a short article supporting Lee Kwan Yew as a future leader for Singapore when at the time some Western politicians were inclined to talk of him as a dangerous left-winger. My short article was published in the *Mercury* in Hobart, for which I received a fee of three guineas.

Margaret remembers Singapore with affection, not least because she was one of a small select group of diplomatic wives who received lessons in Chinese cooking from Mr Lee Kwan Yew's mother. Margaret remembers Mrs Lee as a delightful personality and the lessons for being occasions for the exchange of entertaining gossip. I sometimes feel I should make the distinction between Margaret having lessons in Chinese cooking and actually learning how to cook Chinese food.

Among her many other memories of Singapore Margaret remembers being on the telephone to my secretary when the bomb exploded in Macdonald House where the Australian High Commission was situated and where the Trade Commission was also located. Sadly, two women employees of the Hong Kong and Shanghai Bank on lower floors were killed. Fortuitously no one in the Australian offices was harmed. I say fortuitously because if the bomb had been exploded an hour or two later the blast would have been when at least some children of Australian officials would probably be visiting the building after school hours in company with their mothers. Even more fortuitously I was safely away in Canberra at the time, enjoying dinner at the Hotel Canberra when a message from the Secretary of the Department of Trade and Industry was delivered assuring me that my family had not been affected by the explosion.

The bombing of Macdonald House was an incident during the 'Confrontation' of Malaysia by the Indonesia of President Sukarno. As a keen Royal Australian Navy reservist I was always looking for ways to keep my training record up to date. I learned some significant lessons during three experiences as a watch-keeping officer on the Royal Australian Navy minesweepers that were employed patrolling off Sarawak and in the Malacca Straits. A good experience in a worthwhile cause, an experience complete with its exciting moments and useful lessons, but perhaps a story for another time. The real purpose of this chapter is to explain some of the early lessons I learned about business in Asia and the role of the Overseas Chinese community in the region. An elderly Chinese historian explained to me that over the centuries millions of Chinese had been slaughtered throughout the region, usually as a result of resentment against that community whenever economic conditions worsened. If prices rose, or supplies became short, it was easy to blame the Chinese because they controlled so much of the economic life of the area. The problem continues to arise throughout South East Asia to the present day.

The reason for Chinese predominance in trade in the region is not just their culture of hard work. It is also because they have over the centuries been able to do business in ways that are simply not possible for the different indigenous communities, ways that are also not practicable for most Western businessmen other than for some of those working with multi-national companies. One of my Chinese contacts explained to me how Chinese could do business across the Malacca Straits in ways that no Western trader would dare to deal at a time such as in 1964 when economic conditions in Indonesia were deteriorating rapidly in the final years of Sukarno's rule there.

The secret was, in simple terms, that there were wide family networks that allowed a trader in one city to despatch goods to a member of his wider family in a distant place without having to bother with formalities of credit ratings or letters of credit, the parties to a transaction making adjustments to the details of the formal documentation to meet the needs of the situation. The immediate example was explained to me in the context of Singaporean Chinese firms being able to export general goods to Indonesia at a time when Indonesia had no foreign exchange reserves but did have commodities available for export from one or another of the thousands of islands that make up that country.

From time to time I pass on a simplified explanation of the system as being along the following lines:

Step 1: A young trader in a small port in Sumatra would send a message to an uncle in Singapore saying that he could find a market for a hundred cases of Scotch whisky – certainly not, at least not officially, a priority import.

Step 2: The uncle would send the shipment of whisky from Singapore without any need for letters of credit or bank references. The exporter would phrase the wording and value of the shipping documents in a way that would most easily smooth the goods through import controls at the Indonesian end.

Step 3: The young trader in Sumatra would in turn ship, say, six bales of rubber to a cousin in Hong Kong; again no need for the exporter in Sumatra to worry about credit references or a letter of credit from the importer in Hong Kong.

Step 4: The cousin in Hong Kong would in his turn send a quantity of clothing to another cousin in San Francisco.

Step 5: The cousin in San Francisco would pay the uncle in Singapore for the original shipment of whisky to Sumatra.

The vital part that family networks play in business in South East Asia was brought home to me again in very clear terms twenty years later while I was in Vietnam. I was paying a visit to Singapore and dining with several generations of a Chinese family we had known for many years. I was discussing with the eldest son of the younger generation the fact that Singapore was Saigon's second largest trading partner and that Soviet oil-drilling ships working for the Vietnamese were routinely maintained in Singapore shipyards. Knowing that the family had substantial business interests throughout Asia I asked, 'Is your family doing any business with Saigon?' Without a moment's hesitation the son replied, 'Oh no. All my uncles have left.' No uncles; no business.

The network of trust works very well so long as it can be kept within the wider family circle. In that wider family there are strong loyalties, so that if things go wrong one senior member of the family, an 'uncle', can be counted upon to make good any failing by another member of the family to meet business obligations. The traditional system tends to break down however when a Chinese business expands outside general trading and reaches the stage at which 'outsiders' have to be employed as managers. The problem then is that the outsiders have their own system of loyalties to maintain; such loyalties may take priority over their loyalty to whoever is paying their salary. I would from time to time suggest to a visiting Australian businessman that if he came across an enthusiastic and apparently successful young businessman who was offering a good 'deal', then he, the Australian, should make friendly enquiries about the man's family: if 'no family' then it might be better if it was 'no business', unless of course any business could be backed by impeccable letters of credit.

Another early lesson in Singapore came when I invited two Chinese businessmen to join me for lunch. I quickly discovered that they could talk to each other only in English. The given wisdom is that Chinese is one language with different dialects, yet in practice when it comes to the spoken word the dialects are completely different languages. One of my guests was speaking Cantonese and the other Hokkien. They might as well have been speaking in two languages completely alien to one another. My guests did write a few Chinese characters on a napkin and pass the napkin across the table. Each appeared to understand the characters; though that raises another problem that is still current at the highest levels of business with China itself.

A Chinese character is a drawing, an ideogram. It is in effect a picture intended to convey an idea. At dinner in an excellent Chinese restaurant I asked my Chinese friend of many years standing if he would order the food. Looking at the menu my friend commented that: 'When you read the English language description of a dish you know exactly what you are going to get on the plate; but if you rely on the Chinese language menu you get just a general concept of what the dish might turn out to be.'

Just as we may all look at an artist's painting, especially an abstract work, and each of us see something slightly different from what another person might see in the same painting, so Chinese characters are open to slightly different interpretations. An example of the problem arose quite recently when I was talking informally with a small group of businessmen and lawyers about the matter. One of the lawyers exclaimed that he had had a recent relevant experience. He and some colleagues had been in China negotiating a major contract with a prominent Chinese organisation. As negotiations across the table progressed the lawyer and his clients decided they needed to make some changes to the English language version of the contract. To that end he and his colleagues adjourned to another room where they spent some considerable time changing a word or two and changing some of the punctuation, just to make sure the contract expressed precisely what they understood was being agreed to. The lawyer said that they then went back into the conference room and passed the carefully revised English language contract across the table to the Chinese side. The Chinese representatives took a quick glance at the meticulously revised document and said, 'No need to change the Chinese version.' What precisely were they agreeing to? I sometimes say the situation is rather like Humpty Dumpty telling Alice that: 'A word means just what I choose it to mean.'

Numbers can be another problem, not just with the Chinese business community but with Koreans and others. I would advise businessmen to write any numbers down and put the written numbers in front of whomsoever they were discussing business: and make sure that the decimal point was clearly in the right place! How many English-speakers who are not skilful linguists could instantly and correctly state a complicated number such as 3,200,550 in any Asian language? An English speaker should try asking two Chinese or two Koreans how they would say such a number in their own language: a lengthy exchange would be likely to ensue. There can also be another cultural problem in that there is a tendency for polite Asians to give a foreign visitor whatever number makes the visitor seem happy. Western businessmen and politicians are often quite wide of the mark in understanding the motivations of Asians when it can often be most important to consider the underlying factors rather than just what is said.

In 1964 Margaret and I returned to Australia for me to take up a job in the Department of Trade and Industry on 'shipping matters' for which the most interesting element was being responsible for organising what I believe was the first international conference on the containerisation of cargo. For me it was especially interesting to be involved once more in a subject directly relevant to my years at sea in cargo ships. I did perhaps too well in the task as the successful conference apparently firmly established my reputation with the then Secretary of the Department of Trade, Sir Alan Westerman. I received a message telling me Sir Alan wanted me to write out a job description for myself as a departmental Shipping Adviser. The idea was that I should write out a job description that would very closely match my qualifications and experience but which, just by chance, could not be met by any other individual and certainly not by any existing Australian permanent career public servant. Such a device was at the time the only way the Department of Trade could recruit to senior levels of the permanent Public Service an 'outsider'. Sadly the prospect did not appeal to me at the time and I indicated that I was interested only in remaining a Trade Commissioner. Perhaps my almost immediate appointment as Trade Commissioner to Jakarta was seen as punishment for defying Sir Alan's proposal.

Jakarta proved to be a most worthwhile post for me in several ways. I was not only able to help develop a substantial trade for Australian flour exporters but also to widen my understanding of business in Asia. One lesson was to appreciate the importance of trade marks. The latter led me to emphasise to many Western companies in later years: 'Do what you like to the product but don't change the package.' In such matters I was given a great deal of help and advice by one Indonesian-Chinese in particular: a man who, with his family, has been a good friend for over forty years.

In 1966 and 1967 all foreign diplomats were restricted to west Java, the given reason being that the rest of the country was too dangerous for travel. Diplomats could drive to the Puncak hill country, where most Embassies had one or more 'holiday shacks' in the cooler climate. The Australian embassy had three such weekend retreats and we made good use of them. Living in Jakarta was not too bad so long as you had air-conditioning, but at the time few people, even Australian diplomats, had air-conditioning in any rooms other than the bedrooms.

In spite of the general limitation on travel out of East Java I did make an adventurous journey to what was then known as West Irian (Irian Barat) and now sometimes generally referred to as Indonesian Papua. There was, or at least I considered there was, an Australian commercial interest in the possibilities for Darwin being a major supply base during the construction of the Freeport-MacMoran Grasberg mine, a mine that has become one of the largest gold and copper mines in the world. I applied for a permit to visit the Irian Barat provincial capital, then called Sukarnapura and now Jayapura, to pursue the Australian trade interest. Permission was granted but I was to be accompanied by an official from the Indonesian foreign ministry. He and I turned up at the Jakarta airport only to be told, much to the obvious relief of my Indonesia 'minder', that the flight had been cancelled but should leave the following day. I went home for the night and duly turned up at the airport at the same time the next day. My

Indonesian escort had clearly discovered he had urgent official business elsewhere and did not appear. So I got on the aircraft unescorted. I was the only European on the flight. The plane was a Lockheed Electra that was able to go as far as Biak where the Dutch had maintained, on the site of a wartime US landing field, an airport to service the western half of New Guinea while it remained under Dutch control.

Arriving at Biak I wandered around the crowded airport terminal lobby trying to find out both when there might be a flight on to Sukarnapura and where there might be a hotel at which I could stay until there was such a flight. At this stage it would have been useful to have had my foreign affairs escort with me! Just as I was beginning to wonder what I could do apart from wait indefinitely at the airport, I was accosted by a tall American of impressive bearing who asked me what I was doing there. When I explained that I was going on to Sukarnapura and was looking for a hotel at which to stay until there was an onward flight, he said: 'You can't go there, there is no food. You had better come and stay with us until there is a flight in a day or two.' I then found out that I had been rescued by missionaries!

A group of Protestant churches had an active missionary programme in the Indonesian half of New Guinea, in spite of the Indonesian aversion to any foreigners being in the region at that time. The key to the situation was that the missionaries had aircraft, while the Indonesian military and civil administration had none available. So the missionaries and the military had developed a *modus vivendi* through which the missionaries from time to time flew Indonesian military officers and officials about the territory while in return the missionaries were allowed to continue their Christian missionary work with the local tribes. The group maintained a collective 'R and R' base at Biak, managed by my rescuer at the airport. I have always thought he must surely have been CIA; he certainly did not have about him a personal aura suggesting any particular level of holiness. What better way to be informed of what was going on throughout that wild territory? I had two very interesting days listening to the stories and conversations of the pleasant and dedicated missionaries who came into Biak from the jungle wilderness for a few days' comfort break.

After a couple of days at the missionary base on Biak I, along with sundry Indonesians, chickens, ducks and goats, found a place on a DC3 to Sukarnapura. I arrived in the provincial capital and somehow negotiated transport from the airport to the Governor's office only to find that he had no idea that a foreign diplomat was due to pay a visit. He and his staff were helpful, arranging for me to stay at the government guest-house, while clearly not at all sure what they could do for their unexpected visitor. The government guest-house comprised a row of six timber cabins each containing one room with a simple bathroom. All the cabins opened on to a common balcony. I appeared to be the only guest in residence. The bed was clean and with a mosquito net; but the only food available seemed to be rice and dishes of cabbage. There was no hot water.

It became clear that nothing had been spent on the city since the Dutch departure in 1963. Electricity was available for just two hours a day. A shopping centre was completely derelict and there appeared to be no commercial activity of any kind. It was all very sad. I do not recall seeing any New Guinea tribesmen around the town but the Indonesian officials I met were very friendly, clearly delighted to have a visitor.

I soon realised that the officials in the provincial capital knew little about the plans for the giant copper mine on the south side of the territory. Indeed they had very little to offer by way of information of any kind that might have justified my journey from Jakarta. I quickly became preoccupied with trying to find out how I might get home.

I received an invitation to join a group of civil servants for a game of bridge on the Saturday evening. That experience has allowed me ever since to offer as an excuse for not wanting to play bridge that I have yet to recover from the trauma of playing duplicate bridge by candlelight with twenty-three Minangkabao tribesmen. When I relate this tale to people who know Indonesia they immediately point out the Minangkabao come from west Sumatra, not New Guinea. Quite true. The Minangkabao are a tribe of particularly well-educated, good managers, with a long history of adventurous trade and exploration across the Indian Ocean. My hosts at the bridge evening were a group of government officials virtually exiled by Sukarno to manage Irian Barat, but who in the circumstances of the time were expected to do the managing without any significant wherewithal to do the job and with little support from Jakarta. They had for some years been playing duplicate bridge every Saturday evening and were kind enough to invite me to join them. Their duplicate boards and the playing cards may have been scuffed and worn but their play was excellent! I ended the evening with the lowest score. Just as well we were not playing for even devalued Indonesian money that evening. Most agreeable and hospitable people in spite of the dire straits the region was in at that time.

In the 1960s, before the great copper and gold mine was developed on the south coast, the western half of New Guinea, now called Irian Jaya, had just two exports. The principal export was one tanker load of crude oil every three months from a field operated by Shell. The second largest and only other measurable export was crocodile skins. The Shell interest provided a wonderful oasis in the shape of the Shell manager's house. The Shell manager was a Filipino who, like my bridge playing friends, was pleased to have a fresh face to talk with. Shell looked after their man well in that he not only had a nice house but he also had a generator to provide electricity, together with a supply of Shell diesel fuel to make it work. The Shell manager, who I know was highly regarded by his employers, was a most useful man to talk to about the province's economic activity – or lack of it. He was also the only man in West Irian who could serve a cold beer.

My escape from West Irian was a matter of chance. I had been invited to the Shell manager's house to join him for Sunday lunch. As we were having a pre-lunch cold beer a Volkswagen mini-bus drove up and out of it got three Europeans dressed in smart airline uniforms. They were the pilot, co-pilot, and hostess of the fortnightly Trans Australia Airlines DC3 flight from Lae in east New Guinea. They clearly knew where to come during a brief stop in Sukarnapura. After cheerful greetings the visitors related how, as their flight had approached Sukarnapura, they tried to contact the airport control tower but could get no response. 'But we landed anyway.' They then explained they would be returning to Lae after lunch. 'I'm coming with you,' I said and immediately set about organising transport to pick up my baggage from the government guest-house and get myself to the airport in time for the departing flight. It was all very casual and I have no recollection of what I might have done about buying a ticket – it was long before the days of credit cards – but I do remember there were really no airport formalities. What a relief! I then had to explain to the Department of Trade in Canberra why I was returning to my post in Jakarta by way of Lae, Port Moresby and Brisbane. I could hardly have asked for departmental approval in advance and if I missed that TAA flight it was probable that I had the prospect of being stranded in Sukarnapura for another week if not two. Taking the initiative to go where in independent Indonesia no foreign diplomat had been before, was one more experience from which the lesson was 'don't do it again'.

Among the lessons I learned while in Jakarta was one that I have come to realise applies today in our own Western societies just as much as it did in Indonesia at the time Margaret and I were there in the 1960s. The lesson came to me as I was on my way to lunch in the *kota*, the downtown business district of Jakarta. My companion was a charming elderly Chinese banker.

If Australian exporters were to have any prospect of doing business in Indonesia at a time of critical shortage of foreign exchange it was essential for me to become expert in the frequently changing Indonesia Foreign Exchange Regulations. As my companion and I were driven past the building that housed the Indonesian Central Bank I commented: 'The Central Bank is introducing interesting foreign exchange regulations.' 'Ah yes,' said the Chinese banker. 'Fifty very clever people in the Reserve bank making up these regulations. And down in the *kota* there are five thousand equally clever people working out how to get round them.' We see just that situation everywhere today in our own societies, not just in developing countries. Politicians and bureaucrats with minimal experience of the real outside business world make up new import–export regulations, immigration rules, tax regulations, and new laws for this and new laws for that, without appreciating just how all the new rules might be made to work down in the *kota*. In the world outside politics and bureaucracy, more numerous and perhaps smarter people immediately set to work turning the new rules upside down or simply realise it is safe to ignore them altogether.

One lesson learned in Jakarta came as a real surprise to me, but it was one that helped me greatly in later years, especially when the need came to understand 'Communist' Vietnam at the time I was British Ambassador at Hanoi. This particular lesson came to me unexpectedly at a party.

As Australian Trade Commissioner I had diplomatic rank as Counsellor Commercial at the Australian Embassy. As it so happened that made me at the time second in the Australian Jakarta diplomatic list, though for all practical purposes whenever the Ambassador was away, the Embassy was managed by the senior resident officer from the Department of External Affairs. As mine was the second name on the Australian list of diplomats I received invitations to various national day celebrations at other Embassies. The one national day reception in Jakarta that I remember most vividly was the Austrian celebration. Why I remember it so well had nothing to do with Austria; nor for that matter anything of immediate or direct concern to Australian trade.

The traditional protocol for major events was that a member of an

Ambassador's 'suite' should arrive before his Ambassador. When his Head of Mission arrived he should then make the Ambassador aware of his presence in case it was necessary to convey a message or to receive instructions. Max Loveday was Australian Ambassador to Indonesia at the time. He was someone with whom I got on very well and for whom I had a high regard, but Max did not get directly involved in my commercial work. Nonetheless I made a point of observing the courtesy of arriving early at the reception being held on the lawns of the Austrian residence.

I was standing in the shadow of some large trees that surrounded a floodlit lawn when I found myself unexpectedly face to face with a man who turned out to be a Soviet diplomat. His appearance was almost a caricature of a KGB agent from a James Bond film. 1967 was at the height of the Cold War and this was the first Soviet diplomat I had met – there were none in South Africa and none in Singapore during our time in those countries. I was not at all sure what it was safe to talk about with a Soviet diplomat, or indeed to be seen talking with him at all. More importantly perhaps, not to be seen talking on a one-to-one basis and doing so in the shadows.

There is something of a recitative that diplomats work their way through when they first meet. So I started safely with: 'How long have you been here?' A grunt came back: 'Three months.' Keeping to the script my next line was: 'Where were you before?' Another grunt: 'China.' This was not exactly scintillating or entertaining conversation but I continued the repartee along established lines: 'How long were you there?' An even deeper grunt came back: 'Thirteen years.' At this point I was wondering whether someone from the CIA might be trying to lip-read our conversation in the shadows; so I said to my glum new acquaintance: 'Let us move out into the light a little.' At least I could let people see that my one-on-one conversation with someone who I was certain had to be a KGB man pretending he was a diplomat, was taking place in the open and not surreptitiously among the trees. But just in case someone was lip-reading our exchange I needed to decide what was safe for me to say now in order to continue the dialogue. I quickly thought of a question that I thought was safe and to which my Soviet acquaintance might actually be able to provide a cheerful answer: 'How is the Chinese Communist Party getting on?' The response was immediate and in the form of a contemptuous disgusted grunt: 'The Chinese aren't Communists, they are a nation of petty capitalists.'

Ever since that conversation I have wondered whether if that is what the Soviets thought of Mao's China in 1966 why didn't the West see Chinese communism as a temporary veneer over traditional Chinese society; and subsequently why should the West have been surprised at what has happened in the past thirty years in China? In Vietnam it became increasingly clear that it was nationalism, not Marxist Communist ideology, that drove the Vietnamese.

One trade success during my time in Indonesia was the sale of 5,000 tons of Australian wheat flour, a single order so large that a whole team of flour-mills across three States had to work together to produce the ordered quantity for despatch in a single shipment. This huge sale was at a time when Indonesia had little foreign exchange available and letters of credit in foreign currency issued in Indonesia were little more than a vague promise to make the funds available in twelve months' time. Many years later my good friend Carlo Tabalujan explained how he had been able to persuade the flour-millers to ship the flour.

There was one resident Australian businessman in Jakarta in 1966. He represented the one Australian company that stuck to its Indonesian market through all the difficulties. Ian Murray represented the producers of Aspro, a product that was sold to villagers throughout Java in packets of two tablets at a time. The Aspro sales team travelled around Java in a van that had a projector and screen attached so that they could provide some film entertainment for the villagers as the team worked its way from village to village. Unfortunately for Australian exports there were few companies with the patience or tenacity to develop a market and then persist through difficult times. One Indonesian tried very hard to work with an Australian company to assemble in Indonesia their excellent louvre windows. Such windows had great potential market in a country where there was virtually no air-conditioning and the security environment meant that straightforward open windows were too tempting for someone wanting to enter a building with theft in mind. Although doing very well in Australia the owner of the company did not want to invest in Indonesia the cost of a first shipment of component parts that could then be locally assembled.

The Australian response regarding louvre windows was matched by the short-sightedness of the flour-millers and the Australian Wheat Board when the same Indonesian businessman who had bought 5,000 tons of Australian flour tried hard to convince them to build the first flour-mill in Java. He argued strongly that if they agreed to build a mill Australia would have a monopoly of the supply of flour to Indonesia throughout the construction years and would then have a monopoly of the market for wheat. He got nowhere. Within a few years Singapore Chinese flour-millers built not one but two or three flour-mills. The market for Australian flour was cut off as soon as the Singapore firm entered into the agreement to build the first flour-mill.

Failure to understand Indonesia was not just a failing of businessmen and Western politicians. There were examples of well-meaning but wasted expense in trying to help such countries. Two examples came to notice during my time in Jakarta.

There were reports in the Australian press of starvation on the island of Lombok, the island just to the east of Bali. A well-meaning Sydney housewife announced that she had decided she would do something for the people of Lombok by collecting donations of rice for them. There was then a photograph of this well-meaning person alongside a pile of sacks of rice that were stacked on her suburban veranda.

The next question was how to get the donated rice to the starving people of Lombok. The Indonesians had no money and nor had the well-meaning housewife given any thought as to how to move the rice from her veranda to an island in Indonesia. After some public debate the Royal Australian Air Force agreed to fly the rice to Jakarta as a military transport exercise. The rice duly arrived at Jakarta.

The problem now became that of getting the rice from Jakarta to Lombok. Indonesian infrastructure at the time was in a shambles and neither the Indonesian air force nor any civilian authority had equipment or a budget available for organising such a delivery. It then transpired that there was actually plenty of rice on one end of Lombok while the starvation was at the other end of the island. Transport facilities and mechanisms for moving rice from one end of the island to the other were non-existent in the general chaos of Indonesia at the time. I suspect the rice was eaten in Jakarta, probably by some who could afford to pay for it.

Another example related to American PL480 aid to Indonesia. US Public Law 480 was an interesting scheme to enable countries with serious foreign exchange problems to import food and other essential supplies from the United States but pay for the goods in local currency rather than in US dollars. Or to put it another way it was a scheme to enable American exporters to sell to such countries and receive payment in US government dollars without it appearing that the shipments were actually being given away. The large quantities the US received in what was usually a rapidly devaluing local currency, such as the Indonesian *rupiah*, would then be spent on the local expenses of the US Embassy and whatever other activities the US might be funding in the receiving country at the time.

Under the PL480 scheme a full shipment of American wheat flour arrived in Jakarta. There was no way at the time that US private enterprise could export flour to Indonesia on a commercial basis and expect to be paid in hard currency. US flour millers would however have been happy to see the PL480 shipment disappear over the horizon knowing that they were assured of payment in US currency from their own government. In Tanjong Priok, the port for Jakarta, the flour was unloaded from the ship and stacked on the wharf where it became the responsibility of the Indonesian government. But the Indonesian government had no budget for transport to move the flour and no official experience in distributing wheat flour to whoever might be able to use it to bake bread. The Indonesian government at the time was having enough problems arranging the effective distribution of rice to the population. So the thousands of tons of wheat flour sat on the wharf and went on sitting on the wharf in the humid open air of the port.

After some time the authorities got in touch with my Indonesian-Chinese friend who was the major importer of flour from Australia. They called upon him to use his established network to distribute the American flour among the thousands of small bakeries that his business supplied with flour on a regular basis. The Indonesian government had had to call on a member of the Chinese community to solve their problem. Their need to do so was just one example of how the economies of Indonesia and other countries in South East Asia were, and in many cases still are, dependent on the business skills of the Chinese to keep the wheels of their economies turning. In his autobiography my friend Carlo Tabalujan (Tan Chin Hin – as his name was at the time) relates another example of how the Indonesian government called upon him to solve a large food import problem for them when the Iraqi supplier of dates, a key food item urgently required to arrive before the beginning of Ramadan, would only ship the cargo if my friend personally guaranteed the payment.

Jakarta was a great learning curve for me, one that ensured that I would continue to regard 'doing business in Asia' as a fascinating subject for the rest of my life. What was more immediately important for my future was however a picnic on one of the 'hundred' islands off the coast opposite Tanjong Priok, the port for Jakarta. A family picnic that led to a completely new career.

CHAPTER 2

Joining the FO

A FTER AN ABSENCE OF SIXTEEN years from the United Kingdom I returned to London in 1967 for interviews for an appointment to the Administrative Grades of Her Majesty's Diplomatic Service. The opportunity appeared at a time when I had developed an active interest in any alternative to the Australian Trade Commissioner Service. There was nothing wrong with being a Trade Commissioner. The terms and conditions of service were good and I was proud to be a member of what at the time was certainly the most effective and highly regarded overseas trade promotion service of any government.

The key to the success of the Australian Trade Commissioner Service was, I am certain, that from its establishment in the 1930s almost every Trade Commissioner had had some background in the business world. Perhaps not all had been outstandingly successful in business, and not all might have been brilliant as Trade Commissioners; but whenever an Australian businessman talked to a Trade Commissioner he could be confident that he was talking with someone who had first-hand understanding of commerce and the way businesses worked, rather than talking with a career public servant with no experience of the world outside bureaucracy.

I was however not at all sure that being Trade Commissioner was the ultimate achievement for my career. With Singapore and Jakarta appointments as Trade Commissioner I had already had what I regarded as two of the most interesting and important overseas commercial posts for Australia. I was beginning to wonder what future there was for me for the next twenty-five years. I decided that I had to make a career move then, or perhaps never. So I had begun negotiation with a management consultancy firm in Sydney with the idea of not seeking renewal of my contract when the current one expired in January 1968. It was at that stage, in June 1967, that fate took a hand. My twenty years in Her Majesty's Diplomatic Service came about entirely by a chance reading of a copy of *The Times* while on a picnic.

Not surprisingly I, as Australia's trade representative in Jakarta, had good relations with my British counterpart. Tim Kinnear was then First Secretary

Commercial at the British Embassy. Tim was later Deputy Governor of Bermuda at the time of the murder of that island's Governor. Our paths crossed again when he was Consul General in San Francisco and I was in the same position in Houston. Both the Kinnears and ourselves had young children with us in Jakarta. Tim suggested we hire a boat at Tandjong Priok, the port for Jakarta, and take our families out to one of the 'hundred islands' off the coast for a swim and a picnic. We motored out and anchored just off a glorious little beach which we had entirely to ourselves. Almost thirty years later my wife and I enjoyed a champagne and caviar 'in the surf' party arranged by a small cruise ship, *Sea Goddess II*, on a similarly beautiful island beach off Jakarta – but that is another story.

During the day on the island I felt I was getting a little too much sun, so I waded out to our anchored motor boat and climbed aboard to sit in the shade of the cabin for a while. Tim had brought with him the latest batch of *The Times* newspapers received from London by the British Embassy. Thumbing through one of the papers I came across an advertisement headed 'Late Entry into the Administrative Grades of Her Majesty's Diplomatic Service', for which the key prerequisites were given as '1st class Honours Degree or equivalent and a commercial background'. I tore the advertisement out, folded it and tucked into my shirt pocket.

The Administrative Grades of the Diplomatic Service were traditionally drawn almost exclusively from graduates of Oxford and Cambridge holding first-class degrees in the classics rather than in the 'dismal science' of economics and certainly not in 'trade'. The drive to recruit 'late entrants' into the higher levels of a Service – in which few if any had ever worked in commerce or industry – was clearly one of the early efforts to make the British diplomatic service a little more 'commercial' in its efforts to be more pro-active in helping British exporters.

I certainly did not have a first class honours degree. My Bachelor of Commerce degree from the University of Tasmania, that I had earned as a part-time student, included nothing more significant than a single 'Distinction' in economics. But I was a Chartered Accountant – in qualifying for which I certainly had earned some top marks. I also had an almost completed London University law degree on which I had been working for five years as an external student; and I had eight years at sea in merchant ships involved in international trade. So while it could hardly have been my academic record that led the Civil Service Commission to assume I was the intellectual material they usually recruited for the Administrative Grades of the FO, my previous careers were certainly commercial and included a rather unusual mixture of experiences relevant to international trade.

To my surprise I was invited to London for interviews. I was to get no help with my air fare from Jakarta. However, my mother had died a few months earlier and left me just about enough money to cover a return air fare to London. I hadn't been in England for seventeen years, so a visit would provide me with an opportunity to meet again my brothers and uncles and to visit my parents' grave. I applied for a week's leave to enable me to travel to London for 'personal reasons', the leave being timed to coincide with the dates of the interviews.

The interview process at the Civil Service Commission, then in Sackville Street, was an extremely stimulating experience: three days of tests, interviews and mock committee proceedings, followed by a language aptitude test. I was most impressed and enjoyed the week immensely. On the third day the supervisor told the twenty or so applicants that if they were to be short-listed for the Final Selection Board then they would be so advised in a few weeks' time. At that point I put up my hand and emphasised that I had to return to Jakarta on the Saturday and certainly could not afford to return for another interview. At the conclusion of the language test the following day, Thursday, I was told to appear before a Final Selection Board to be held the next day. So I had the unusual circumstance of being given my own personal Final Selection Board, set up at twenty-four hours' notice so that I could go through the whole process in one week. That might be a record for the selection process. I can only assume that I must have made something of a favourable impression for the Civil Service Commission to be able to gather together at such short notice the appropriate group of senior people for a final interview! I remember virtually nothing of the interview except being seated at one end of a long table.

I sometimes relate that it later dawned on me that there was one particular qualification that may have tipped the scales in my favour. As I really didn't expect to be offered a job I felt I had nothing to lose by being quite open and even rather daring in my analysis of the files and situations presented to each candidate for analysis and a decision. I remember particularly one set test that described a situation in which there was a terrorist incident in a Latin American country just before the Duke of Edinburgh was due to make a visit to open a British trade fair. The hypothetical situation required advice as to whether the Duke's visit should go ahead or be immediately cancelled. Being full of courage in a situation in which I would have no actual responsibility, I argued that the Duke should indeed continue to plan to visit the country concerned rather than let it be said the British were 'chicken' in the face of a single terrorist act that was in any event not specifically aimed at Britain or things British. Perhaps my robust approach to the matter demonstrated a favoured British stiff upper lip – at least in a situation in which I was not personally at risk.

One of the sessions in the interview process required each candidate to be self-critical and explain what he considered to be his own major weakness. In all honesty, and some nerve, I wrote that I considered my major failing to be that I was fundamentally a very lazy person. The following day included a one-to-one session with a psychologist. The psychologist said to me that my self-evaluation as a lazy person could not be true because of all the things I had done. From then on I have maintained that psychologists do not understand the real nature of the truly lazy man. In my view the truly lazy man, rather than a merely indolent one, is to be compared with the devout Hindu or Buddhist whose whole objective in life is to reach the ultimate goal of nirvana, or nothingness; but who in his search for that state of bliss works like a slave all his life, travelling hopefully without ever quite reaching his objective.

At the end of a very stimulating week in London I returned to Jakarta and told Margaret that I didn't mind if I wasn't offered a job. The interview process was so intellectually stimulating and interesting that it was itself worth the air fare. I learned later that an active 'positive vetting' was carried out, the Australian federal security organisation carrying it out on behalf of the British. Fortunately I had a group of very good and highly respected friends in Hobart, particularly in the legal community of the day!

The problem came when I was indeed offered employment as a member of Her Majesty's Diplomatic Service. I was presented with a decision that was really the greatest gamble I have ever made. The position offered meant a drop in salary as well as a drop in rank from Counsellor equivalent in the Australian Trade Commissioner Service to starting as a First Secretary in the British Diplomatic Service. In addition I had to meet at my own expense the full cost of transferring my wife and four children from Australia to Britain. I also had to re-establish our four children in English schools. To avoid yet a further change of school for the older children we had to get them in to good boarding schools in England as soon as possible and then meet the full cost of school fees until such time as I was confirmed in my appointment and received an overseas posting. There would be no 'allowances' of any kind until I received that first overseas posting, an event that would in itself be dependent upon me satisfactorily completing a period of probation. It was by far the greatest gamble I have ever made. I have no complaint about the system. It certainly tested my determination to make a career as a diplomat rather than just in 'Trade'!

Before I left Hobart for London I put together 'Doing Business in Indonesia: a guide for Australian businessmen'. I had offered to give up my final leave entitlement to do a de-briefing for Australian businesses around Australia but the Department were perhaps a bit miffed at me leaving and declined my offer. I thought it would be too much of a waste not to pass on the knowledge and understanding I had of business in Indonesia, so I spent the period of leave writing my 'guide'. I sold 700 copies and accompanied it with a number of 'free' seminars I organised myself in several of the State capitals. I made just enough from the exercise to pay my air fare to London.

The family move to London was made in best diplomat style. I flew to London to arrive a couple of days before my scheduled start date at the Foreign Office and left Margaret to 'pack and follow'.

CHAPTER 3

London: 1968–69

ON 8 MARCH 1968, I ARRIVED in King Charles Street for my first day
with Her Majesty's Diplomatic Service. I expected to be put through
a lengthy induction course similar to the three months of 'training' that
began my six years with the Australian Trade Commissioner Service. Not
a bit of it. I was greeted by an official who looked down a list he was
holding and said words along the lines of: 'Ah, Tallboys. Yes. East Africa
Department: Desk Officer for Kenya, Uganda and the East African
Economic Community; go away and do it.' This was I suppose in the best
British tradition that if a person was intelligent enough to be appointed to
the Administrative Grades then he must be intelligent enough to do any
job without delay!

The 'Third Room' environment of a Foreign & Commonwealth Office
department was in practice a very effective 'on the job' training experience.
Working in the 'Third Room' were two First Secretary desk officers and a
Second Secretary, each with different but related fields of work, which
meant that they were not each working in isolation but could discuss across
the large central table the issues of the day, bouncing ideas around. It
seemed to me to be a most effective arrangement. It was also a
companionable environment in which to work: one got to know colleagues
with different experiences and different backgrounds.

The two who were with me in the Third Room of East Africa
Department were an experienced Executive Grade First Secretary and a
bright young twenty-plus something who was an Executive Grade Second
Secretary. They were both sensible people who helped me along in my
early days in what was for me a brand new working environment. I enjoyed
my first spell of working in the FCO in Whitehall and gained a good feel for
the way the system worked at Desk level. The experience came in useful
when I returned to Whitehall as an Assistant Head of Department sitting in
my own office somewhat remote from the department's Third Room.

My first assignment in the Diplomatic Service was by no means commercial
in nature, which of course suited me very well indeed. The particular 'desk'

I had been allocated was however logical enough in view of my brief Kenya experience as Acting Australian Trade Commissioner at Nairobi in 1962. The East African Economic Community component of my 'brief' did provide an element of commercial work, and economics came into the consideration of what the future for the three East African territories might be as independent countries. My earlier experience in Nairobi had provided me with an appreciation of the tribal and other issues that were relevant to understanding the tensions in both newly independent African countries and in the East African territories about to become independent. In 1968 East Africa Department had to deal with the political problems of the early stages of the Asian exodus from Uganda. The Asian community played in East African business life much the same role that the Chinese communities have for centuries played in South-East Asia. Without the Asian skills and culture of hard work the economies of Kenya and Uganda were to suffer.

Few in the Indian community in East Africa wanted to return to India while at the same time India didn't want them to return and thus add to the unemployment and other social problems India was having to cope with at the time. At the same time the British Labour government was having difficulty in settling a firm policy about the admission into Britain of the Asian families being driven out of East Africa. Officials in London were having to deal with a prominent activist, Mr Praful Patel, and others, without being able to give a clear indication as to what British government policy was or would be. The subject led to heated discussions in the 'Third Room' of East Africa Department about immigration in general. In the middle of one such discussion it was the most junior of the three in the room, the girl from Yorkshire, who burst out with the remark, 'But we are all immigrants!' That stopped us in mid-argument, as we recognised that that is in fact true of the great majority of people who think of themselves as English: waves of immigrants over the centuries, from Danes to Normans and on to the Huguenots with more recent additions of displaced people fleeing Nazi rule, not to forget the Scots, the Irish and the Welsh contributed to creating English society as we knew it in the 1960s. What exactly is an Englishman?

An interesting experience of my time as Desk Officer in East Africa Department was assisting the Kenya government make provisional plans for a state funeral for Jomo Kenyatta. The matter was extremely delicate and given a security classification to reflect that delicacy. President Kenyatta was still very much alive. In the United Kingdom the Lord Chamberlain's office has had centuries of experience at contingency planning for sudden deaths of the monarch and other members of the Royal Family. Those at the head of a mature Western government might appreciate the need for such planning, but to be discovered to be planning the funeral of the President of a newly independent African nation could well be misunderstood in government circles in such a country. Such activity might be seen as a step towards 'plotting' the death of the country's leader.

As there was no precedent for such an event in independent Kenya it was sensible to have a contingency plan drawn up by experts, especially as there was at the time some concern about President Kenyatta's health. It was understandable that those recognising the need for such planning should turn to London for advice from those with experience of such matters. The intention was that Kenyan officials could be sure they had detailed workable plans that could be acted upon at very short notice. Contact with the Foreign and Commonwealth Office on this delicate matter was made in the person of the Kenyan Minister of Agriculture, Bruce MacKenzie. MacKenzie was the one white minister in the Kenya government of the time.

My role involved acting as liaison with the Lord Chamberlain's Office in St James's Palace and with the leading firm of undertakers. The Lord Chamberlain was asked to provide advice on matters of ceremony and protocol for a State funeral, while the undertakers were to provide guidance on such matters as care of the body and also to have ready plans for expert embalmers and others to fly immediately to Nairobi when called upon to do so.

I had several very pleasant morning walks through St James's Park in execution of my part in planning Kenyatta's funeral arrangements. I always tried to arrange my appointments with the Lord Chamberlain's Office so that they coincided with the Changing of the Guard. In due course I received a personal letter of appreciation from Bruce McKenzie for the assistance I gave to his emissary, Colonel Anderson, in making the necessary plans. As it happened, Jomo Kenyatta – undoubtedly the best President independent Kenya has had – went on for a further ten years. McKenzie was killed much earlier in a suspicious aircraft crash.

Margaret and the twins arrived in London a month or two after I started in Whitehall. They travelled by sea, thereby allowing them to board ship in Hobart with rather more luggage than would have been possible if they had travelled by air. Roger and Pru followed later by air at the end of a school term. Roger was in his second year at Geelong Grammar and Prudence was at Clyde School, also in Victoria. For them the switch to the English education system was by no means easy. We had considerable difficulty in choosing what we thought would be the right schools for them, bearing in mind that until I received an overseas posting I would get no help towards boarding-school fees. The more prominent public schools such as Westminster, Sherbourne, and others that I approached were generally very receptive to the idea of having a new pupil transferring from Geelong Grammar; but each wanted to know about Roger's standard in Latin. As Geelong students for the most part dropped Latin after just one year, that meant we made no progress with such schools. As so often happens after what is an initial disappointment, being turned down by such schools in itself turned out to be a 'good thing'.

Someone suggested we talk to David Emms, at that time headmaster at Cranleigh School. Emms was considered 'progressive' and was establishing a growing reputation for that 'young' nineteenth century public school. Emms responded positively and said that he would take Roger providing he was doing well in other subjects. He advised us to send him first to Holmewood House preparatory school for a year, even if that meant Roger would be a little older than the average age of those starting in the Cranleigh senior school. The then headmaster of Holmewood House, Baramian, was considered something of a wizard at getting boys into good public schools. We were sufficiently well impressed with Roger's experience at Holmwood House that we sent Peter there later. We entered Peter at two or three 'top' public schools but Cranleigh did such a good job educating Roger that we sent Peter to follow him there also.

We discovered that selecting schools for girls was not so easy. It was at a time when a number of boarding schools were closing for lack of support. Pru eventually went to Priorsfield. The Priorsfield connection to the Huxley family suggested to us that the academic standard would be good. Furthermore, a school with a married woman as headmistress seemed to us to offer an excellent balance for a girl whose parents would be living abroad. We had to make the decision in a hurry and found out only later that the school and its headmistress were both entering a period of crisis. Pru nonetheless survived and turned out to have aptitudes and skills that Priorsfield failed to develop. We had better luck when the time came to send Sarah 'home' to boarding school, sending her first to Sibton Park near

Folkestone and then to St James's at West Malvern. St James's 'assessment' of Sarah proved to be very apposite. It is easy to forget that in the 1960s and 1970s there was almost no boarding school that took both boys and girls. In any event we were of the view that it was best to separate the twins at school rather than risk them becoming too dependent on each other.

We felt that boarding school meant that our children retained the stability that went with continuity of school environment, continuity of teachers and of school friends. At the same time they came to us and together for two or three school holidays each year to spend time in a house where there were numerous familiar items, such as books, that they associated with being 'at home'. But this is an issue for personal decision.

If parents do not like the idea of boarding school yet their working career leaves little alternative but to send their children away to school, then I do believe it to be of utmost importance that the parents must not allow their dislike of boarding school to be apparent to their children. If Mummy cries when saying goodbye to little Johnny or Mary as they depart for a first long journey to school, then the evidence that Mummy clearly thinks boarding school is a bad thing may immediately be engraved on the child's mind. The initial impression that boarding school is surely going to be an awful and unhappy experience that reduces a mother to tears, is perhaps certain to be confirmed for the child in reality. On the other hand it seems to have worked for our family. In time it came about that the four came to live in four separate countries with one twin in London and the other in New Zealand; yet they all talk to each other almost every week and our daughters are fortunate in having very supportive brothers.

Apart from organising schools and finding the wherewithal to pay the fees, there was the matter of finding rented accommodation for a large family. We thought it would be a good idea to have the experience for a year or two of living in the English countryside as far out from London as was compatible with a daily commute to Whitehall. Living at Mereworth in rural Kent certainly had its good points, at least at weekends; but I soon realised that thirty minutes frantic driving through country lanes to get to Tonbridge Station in order to catch the right train to Charing Cross, and then not getting home until eight o'clock in the evening, was not something I would wish to do for more than a year or so.

I took the opportunity during the first few months in London, before we moved to the country, to finish off my Bachelor of Laws degree at the

University of London, making use of the library at Senate House and sitting the final examination with several hundred others at Crystal Palace in June 1968. I then enrolled as a student at Lincoln's Inn and started to sit my 'dinners'. This seemed a sensible thing to do, just in case the Diplomatic Service decided after all I was not quite want they wanted. But after twelve months, rather than the specified eighteen months on 'probation' as a Desk Officer at the FCO that I had been led to expect, I received notice of my first overseas posting together with my first overseas and education allowances.

It was just as well that the news of the appointment to Brasilia came when it did. By then Margaret and I almost certainly did not have enough savings left to get the family back to Australia if I had been rejected for permanent appointment! The only negative aspect was that having sat almost two terms of dinners at Lincoln's Inn I was at the time so hard up that I felt I had no alternative but to turn in my Lincoln's Inn student card in order to recover the £100 deposit. As is often the case, we from time to time regret the things we didn't do. I would have thoroughly enjoyed being a barrister. As a barrister manqué I now have to be content with television courtroom dramas such as *Kavanagh QC*.

My posting to Brasilia began an unusual succession of postings as a member of Her Majesty's Diplomatic Service.

CHAPTER 4

Brasilia: 1969–72

B RASILIA, THE CAPITAL OF BRAZIL in the central area of the country, was formally inaugurated on 22 April 1960. Just five years before, the area had resembled a desert, with few people, scarce water, few animals and few plants. The project was the dream of President Juscelino Kubitschek, who became President in 1956. Kubitschek's vision was that by creating a capital in the centre of the country Brazilians would be encouraged to invest in developing the interior instead of sending their money off to Europe. The outcome was perhaps more than Kubitschek envisaged. The success of his project in its attraction to the interior of large numbers of people and large amounts of money, was the single most important factor leading not just to the development of the semi-arid *sertao* but also to the opening up of the Amazon forests to 'development'.

There were certain anomalies about the planning and architecture of the country's capital. In a predominantly Catholic country the cathedral in Brasilia was designed by the communist Oscar Niemeyer. The renowned Brazilian town planner Lucio Costa had lost his wife in a motor car accident and had declared that he would design a city where there would be no need for traffic lights: a city that would be free of serious road accidents. Within ten or so years of its founding, road casualties in Brasilia were exceeding those in Rio – primarily, it would appear, because the long straight arterial road through the centre of the city, together with the distances to the outer suburbs, encouraged driving at high speeds. Nonetheless it was an agreeable city at the time that we were there; not least because it attracted little attention from official or other visitors.

In Brazil my appointment was as 'First Secretary in Charge' of the British Embassy establishment in the new capital. This was at a time when Sir David Hunt, the Ambassador, together with all other more senior officers, were still based in Rio de Janeiro. It soon became clear that Sir David and his wife Iro had every intention of staying in Rio for as long as possible.

Britain had been one of the first countries to spend large sums of money on staff accommodation in Brasilia before it was realised that the Brazilian Foreign Ministry *Itamarati* were themselves in no hurry to move from Rio to the semi-arid *sertao* in the centre of their own country. The capital is built around a central artifical lake, Laka Paranoa, and Britain had built five houses for senior officers on the *Peninsula do Sul* at one end of the lake and another house intended for an Embassy Minister – 'Deputy Head of Mission' – on the *Peninsula do Norte* at the other end. The two elements of senior staff residential accommodation could not have been further apart from each other or further away from the site of the intended Chancery and ambassadorial residence on the Avenida das Nações. The separation of the residences for Embassy senior officials was almost certainly because the Peninsula do Norte, across the lake from the presidential palace – the Palace of the Dawn – was designated as a residential area for 'higher' officials while the Peninsula do Sul was for middle-class officials and private residents.

An ugly block of staff apartments had also been built. This accommodation had the advantage of at least being much closer to the Chancery site. The staff block was disliked by the Brazilians because of its almost 'Stalinist' appearance, not at all in keeping with the modern architecture of all the other apartment blocks. Furthermore the British Ministry of Works had constructed a building that was designed to be earthquake proof, doing so in a part of Brazil that was considered to be the area most likely in the whole of South America to be safe from earthquakes. So much was Brasilia considered to be earthquake-free that the British Geological Society had chosen an area close to Brasilia as the best place in the continent at which to construct an earthquake monitoring system.

The five houses on the southern peninsula remained for many years almost the only buildings on that peninsula. They were not occupied by anyone from the Embassy until after Margaret and I had left Brazil. One of my recurring worries while in Brasilia was that a journalist from a newspaper such as the *Sunday Express* would drop in and discover just how much taxpayers' money had been spent on buildings that remained unoccupied for nearly ten years. It was just as well that journalists as well as diplomats preferred to stay in Rio. I cannot recall a single journalist visiting us during the two and a quarter years I was Head of Post in the capital, though our guest book indicates that someone from the *Yorkshire Post* must have been entertained by us. Whatever had attracted a representative of the *Yorkshire Post* to the capital he was obviously not that curious about the Embassy properties and I certainly was not going to draw his attention to the five houses sitting in isolated splendour on the outer peninsula of the city.

The early permanent structures that had been built for the Embassy were by 1969 all something of an embarrassment for one reason or another. The temporary Chancery building on the Avenida das Nações on the other hand was charming and a delight for us to live in for the first year and a half of our posting. It was rather like a *Beau Geste* oasis in the semi-desert. The site was at the time different from any neighbouring block in 'Embassy Row' in that almost all the other blocks of land allocated for embassies had been left in their untended natural state. The only other permanent diplomatic structures in Brasilia in 1969 had been built by the United States and Czechoslovakia. The British site was outstanding in that its modest but pleasantly designed temporary building was surrounded by a garden that had had ten years of steady watering: so different from the surrounding *sertao* that the vegetation had attracted a variety of birds and other wild life, including a few snakes.

We had at our disposal a tennis court and a temporary swimming pool was soon added to make us the envy of the six or seven other countries that had an established presence in Brasilia at the time. The Czech Embassy permanent building was occupied by a most agreeable but lonely Second Secretary, Jindrich Tucek, while the only resident Ambassadors in our time were those from India and Guyana; all were delightful colleagues. The Indian Ambassador was an army general; while the Ambassador for Guyana, Evan Drayton, was a political appointee who lost his job when there was a change of government in the country he was representing.

The United States, needless to say, had a much larger presence than any other country, even though their Ambassador was, like Sir David Hunt, staying in Rio for as long as was diplomatically possible. The American Brasilia outpost included a few Marines whose Marine Ball provided the main social event of the year for all of us.

On my very first posting for HM Diplomatic Service I was already in charge of my own post – something for which many colleagues waited many years. I enjoyed the whole experience immensely. As far as the Brazilians were concerned the capital was the most important centre for their international affairs interests; at least that was so once their own Foreign Ministry had moved from Rio. There were only four other home-based British staff in Brasilia when we arrived, one of whom being from the Ministry of Works; but the job and the staff establishment for which I was responsible began to expand as more Brazilian ministries moved to the new capital. It was an early experience that suggested that

many embassies gathered staff and expenditure regardless of whether there
was much real business to be done.

Brasilia was a most agreeable posting for us as a family. The older
children had by then started at boarding school in England but came 'home'
for school holidays. Brasilia, although designated a hardship post, actually
had a healthy and agreeable climate. The children were able to swim at the
Clube do Iate throughout the year. Playing golf was a bit tricky however as
the rough on the then nine-hole course was infested with snakes. A very
far-sighted predecessor of mine had bought two shares in the *Clube de Golfe*
when it was first established. I took over the shares and in due course passed
them on to someone else. I suspect that in later years a First Secretary at
the Embassy had to surrender his membership to a more senior member of
the staff.

Preparations for the inevitable move of the whole of the diplomatic corps
led to me having responsibility for supervising a variety of construction work
expanding the temporary Chancery buildings, as well as direct involvement
in a whole range of administrative matters that service in large posts might
not have provided to an officer in the 'political' stream of the Service.

The situation in Brasilia meant that I was dealing with the politics of the
Brazilian Congress as well as, before long, with the whole range of issues
that required Embassy contact with the Foreign Ministry. Indeed, because
I was so frequently in and out of the doors of the *Palacio d'Itamariti* visiting
various departments in the Foreign Ministry, the security officials there
seemed to recognise me more easily than they recognised some of their
own Brazilian diplomats. I do not recall ever being asked to produce a
security pass when I entered the building. Brazilians occasionally referred
to me as *O mini embaixador.*

Social life tended to be very much a matter between those embassies with
staff permanently in the capital and with Brazilian diplomats and officials of
the few government departments already in the city. There was very little
cultural life and we looked forward each week to attending the government
cinema where films were shown by the film censors before general release
to the public. The Vice-President, a Brazilian admiral, was a regular
member of the audience at the weekly censors' film show, where we did
see a number of films that were certainly not going to be released for
general showing to the Brazilian population during the military regime of
President Medici. Apart from one or two films showing a little more 'sex'
than was felt suitable for ordinary Brazilians, I remember *Battleship Potemkin*

as an unusual presentation, one of those famous films I am pleased to have seen but would not have left home on a winter's evening to view at a public cinema.

Entertainment being limited there was considerable delight when the first commercial cinema was about to open, especially when it was advertised that the first film to be shown would be Zefforelli's *Romeo and Juliet*. Margaret and I were delighted when we received our invitation to the formal opening of the cinema, to be attended by President Medici. It was a rare occasion not just to dress up for an evening but also to look forward to what we anticipated would be some sophisticated cultural entertainment.

On the night of the opening, a rare 'black tie' occasion for Brasilia of that time, there was the usual formality on such occasions with all guests being seated before the President arrived. All those present then stood for the national anthem and, as the lights in the auditorium were lowered, we sat down with great anticipation for the opening of *Romeo and Juliet*. What came up on the screen was John Wayne in *True Grit*. It was apparently a personal choice of President Medici. No accounting for taste; but nonetheless a good film.

Manuel Mendez, Editor of the *Correio Brasiliense* newspaper, was a good friend to the foreign diplomats in Brasilia. It was always a highlight of social life to be invited out to his *fazenda* for a Sunday *churrasco* lunch. His property was some distance out of Brasilia, well beyond the benefit of any irrigation from the city lake. The grounds of his weekend 'shack' provided us with an introduction to just what the semi-desert of the *sertao* was really like in its natural condition before irrigation was available.

It was Manuel Mendez who explained to us that Brazilians had had no success in growing fruit and vegetables in the vicinity of the new capital. It was seen that there would be increasing difficulty in supplying fresh food to the rapidly growing population of the city and its surrounding suburbs. Members of the Brazilian Korean community were encouraged to move to the area to try their hand at market-gardening; but they failed and it seems that the Korean pioneers into the interior ended up as local shopkeepers. Then the Japanese community were induced to move in. The Japanese made such a success of horticulture in the area that by the time we were in Brasilia the region was exporting produce to cities further south.

Manuel Mendez, as one might expect from a newspaper editor, was a good source of information on a number of aspects of Brazilian life, including the place of *macumba* in a generally very Catholic society. The general impression we gained was that many Brazilians hedged their bets by going to mass on Sundays and to a *macumba* ceremony on Thursdays. For many Brazilians *macumba* was 'white' rather than 'black' magic, but nonetheless a real force in life. The American Principal of the International School had made a special study of *macumba* and gave occasional lectures on the subject to the small international community. Our younger children were attending the International School when we received advice that the headmaster had left Brasilia suddenly. The story was that he had got too close to his subject and had been receiving ominous hints that perhaps he should go away. On more than one occasion when driving through the undeveloped area of the diplomatic quarter early in the morning I would approach a deserted crossroads to see a dead cockerel in the middle of the junction together with empty *cachaça* bottles pointing outwards to the four principal points of the compass. I convinced myself that these significant symbols were not directed at me personally. I did not stop to inspect closely.

One of Margaret's good Brazilian friends was the wife of the local Air Force commander Brigadier Eppinghous. The names of the Brigadier and his wife appear in our guest book on the dates for more than one of our dinner occasions. He was a popular and highly regarded individual who was expected to go higher in the Brazilian Air Force. Soon after we left Brasilia our friend died in a mysterious air crash. The story that came to us was that a person who was not opposed to the Brigadier personally but who wanted him to 'move on' from Brasilia in order to create a vacancy for another air force officer, had consulted with the practitioners of *macumba* to arrange appropriate spells that they thought would ensure the Brigadier went to another appointment. According to the story there had been no wish to bring about the good man's death! The spells had apparently got out of control. Believe it or not?

Embassy personnel based in Rio complained to me on occasion that in Rio they had hardly any opportunity to practise speaking Portuguese because the sophisticated society of Rio spoke English and liked to practise their knowledge of it. In Brasilia on the other hand I had to speak Portuguese. I soon discovered that many of the Brazilian government officials, let alone ordinary citizens, spoke no English at all. I was good enough at it to manage an occasional radio and television interview. The sad thing is of course that if you do not continue to practise a skill you lose it.

One of my press interviews related to the problem of the Tupamaros guerrillas – 'terrorists' in later terminology. This group had taken to kidnapping senior foreign diplomats, including, if I remember correctly, the American Ambassador in Rio, and actually killing the British Ambassador to Uruguay. The security scare suggested that a possible target might be whatever diplomat might be in charge of the British Embassy establishment in the capital – for which read Me! So two-way radios were installed in the Embassy official car and Margaret was issued with her personal mace spray.

I am not sure that either security step would have been much good if an attack took place but the moves were no doubt intended to show that higher levels in the Diplomatic Service cared for us. For a time the tension was real. The sequel was that when we left Brasilia for Phnom Penh, and immediately found ourselves in the middle of a shooting war, I relaxed. I rationalised the change on the basis that in Brasilia any young Brazilians hanging about outside our accommodation at night might just be planning something nasty for me personally, whereas none of the artillery, bombs and tracer bullets that we could hear and see from our bedroom balcony in Cambodia were actually aimed at us. Nothing personal in all that drama around Phnom Penh: it would be just bad luck if a rocket came in through the bedroom window.

We had some, but not many visitors. A party from the Royal Geographical Society came through Brasilia on their way to inspect a site they had marked off a year earlier as being a square mile of country that had not previously been touched by humans. We took the opportunity to send our son Roger off into the jungle with them for a week or so as an adventure that might give him inspiration for a scientific career. The experience did not imbue him with any continuing interest in either exploration or uncomfortable adventures. When the RGS party passed through Brasilia on their way back to Europe they told us that by the time they made their second visit to the pristine jungle location, just twelve months after the first visit, there was a weekly bus service passing by the site.

Sir Anthony Blunt visited and our guest book suggests that he stayed overnight with us on 10–11 August 1970. Just why the Keeper of the Queen's Pictures should visit Brasilia I cannot recall. It was only some years later that we realised that the signature in our guest book was that of the Fourth Man in the Philby, Maclean, Burgess spy saga. We remember him as a man of rather dull personality.

Robin Hanbury-Tenison stayed briefly on his way to an expedition into the Mato Grosso and years later he and I were together as guest lecturers on a cruise ship. The Singapore Foreign Minister, Rajaratnam, paid a visit. As there was no Singapore representation in Brasilia my wife and I hosted a reception for him. Not long after we left Brasilia Margaret stopped over in Singapore and went to a large dinner-party hosted by a friend. When she sat down at the table she and her neighbour felt they had met before. Her neighbour was Rajaratnam. Like all Ministers in the Singapore government Rajaratnam was a first class person. Some Ambassadors from Rio called and appear in our guest book, including the Australian: in those days there was hardly anywhere else for them to be entertained if they were staying overnight in the capital. We offered modest hospitality to a number of other visitors but much of the entertaining we did was of Brazilians and of the few other diplomats already established in the city.

Among the Brazilians, Margaret made particular friends with Donna Passarinho, wife of the Minister of Education. Margaret met regularly with Donna Passarinho and a group of her friends. The Minister himself was much respected and something of an anglophile. He seemed to feel particularly badly about summoning me to his office to complain about left-wing bias in the BBC Portuguese language service broadcasting to Brazil, asking me to urge the BBC to look closely at the background of their Portuguese language broadcasters. The Minister's complaint was that some of the broadcasters had a nasty habit, as he saw it, of giving emphasis to what they were reading in such a way as to provide the material with a particularly anti-Brazilian government twist.

There was some difficulty in getting one's Brazilian guests to arrive on time for a set dinner. 'Dinner at Eight' was better expected to be closer to 'Dinner at Ten'. It was possible to give some emphasis to timing by annotating the invitations with '*hora inglesa*', a term Brazilians used when wishing to convey some idea that timing was important. But that didn't always work. On the other hand the Brazilians had neat ways of indicating the dress to be worn for a function: '*a vontade*' has a more elegant tone about it than 'casual' or 'as you please'.

Our Brazilian friends were great party people. It was at the Foreign Minister's home at Carnival time in 1972 that I last danced the *samba* until dawn. All the energy used in dancing the *samba* meant that I did not suffer any ill after-effects from the numerous *caiparinhas* and *batidas di limao* that I consumed during the party.

Being Head of Post meant that we had a full social life but with just a sprinkling of British guests. My own Ambassador kept away from the city, perhaps to avoid giving London any impression that his presence in the capital might be of some importance. I thought it also possible that in support of his own preferences Sir David did not want to send his senior officers on regular visits to the capital in case the increase in travel expenditure came to the notice of London and led to enquiries as to whether it was time for the Embassy to move. A regular stream of visits by his Minister and Counsellors might have led to Sir David being urged to speed up arrangements for his own transfer to Brasilia in view of the thus evident increase in Embassy business to be transacted in the capital.

By 1969, when we arrived in Brasilia, the Presidency, the Vice-Presidency, the Congress, and two or three government ministries were already established in the capital. In 1970 the Brazilian Foreign Ministry, *o Itamarati*, transferred from Rio.

I always knew that HM Ambassador at the time, Sir David Hunt, was a man with a brilliant intellect, and not just because he stayed in Rio and left all the important Embassy business to me in Brasilia. After retirement Sir David twice became Mastermind of the Year on BBC television, his expertise being, if I remember correctly, ancient Greek history. Greek history would not however perhaps have been the ideal study background for later diplomats required to think much more along the lines of the business community's interest in trade.

On one of his rare visits to Brasilia Sir David made a comment that certainly gave me something to think about. During a long conversation while we waited for dinner to be served at what was at the time the nearest thing Brasilia could claim as a 'sophisticated' restaurant, Sir David mentioned that he had been Private Secretary to both Prime Minister Attlee and to Prime Minister Churchill. Sir David related the well known details of Churchill's work practices and then said that he found 'Attlee to be a better decision maker than Churchill'. I puzzled over that remark for time until I realised that Sir David had been Private Secretary when Winston Churchill was a peace-time Prime Minister; he was not referring to Churchill's decision making capacity as a war-time Prime Minister. I see Sir David's comment illustrating an example of a man who is a great leader in time of war and danger, a time for 'blood, sweat and tears', but who does not necessarily make such an effective leader in times of peace.

In the two and a half years of my time as Head of Post in the Brazilian capital Sir David made just four visits to the city. The first occasion was a few weeks after we had arrived. Sir David was himself a recent arrival in Brazil and had no alternative but to come to the capital to present his credentials to President Medici at the *Palacio d'Alvorado*, the 'Palace of the Dawn'. Sir David's second visit was to attend the celebrations at the *Palacio d'Itamariti* to mark the transfer of the Brazilian Foreign Ministry from Rio. The *Palacio d'Itamariti* was in my opinion easily, inside and out, the most attractive and well designed of the buildings in the new capital. What is more the Brazilian Foreign Ministry's diplomats certainly knew how to put on a good party! There was however one negative experience of the evening. We must have been stuck for at least twenty minutes in the incredible traffic jam outside the building while the long line of Ambassadors and other dignatories in their limousines slowly approached the point at which they could alight to enter the front entrance of the brand new building and be greeted by the Foreign Minister. That experience did suggest that in spite of all its ultra–modern planning Brasilia might be in for some horrific traffic problems in the future.

Sir David's third visit was arranged while I was on mid–tour leave but the visit itself took place after I had returned. It was, I imagine, thought that the Ambassador ought to be seen to be conducting some foreign policy business in the capital. My recollection is that nothing worthwhile was accomplished.

Sir David's fourth visit to Brasilia was to highlight the formal transfer of himself and the Embassy from Rio de Janeiro. A second purpose was to say good–bye to Margaret and to me. I had persuaded London that it would be difficult for me to stay on when more senior officers would be in post while most Brazilian officials would prefer to speak to the individual they had got to know personally as the representative of Britain in the capital. I thought it would be good for my career if I moved on.

The Brazilians were getting rather fed up with the delays in embassies moving to the capital and eventually set September 1972 as the date by which all ambassadors had to transfer themselves from Rio to Brasilia. The incentive was that any ambassador who had not moved his embassy to the capital by that date would lose his diplomatic privileges. Ambassadors could not be deprived of their diplomatic immunity if they chose to continue living in Rio, but they could lose their duty–free whisky. That certainly got them moving. Life in Rio, combined with a continuing consular privilege of duty free liquor, was such an attraction that one Latin American ambassador, the Guatamalan I believe it was, had himself downgraded to Consul General so that he and his wife, together with her dress-shop, could stay in Rio. The malicious gossip, quite unfounded I am sure, was that significant quantities of duty free whisky leaked out through the back door of the dress-shop.

On that fourth visit Sir David and Lady Hunt stayed in Brasilia just long enough to serve us a farewell drink before they returned to the airport to fly back to Rio on the same day that Margaret and I departed the city for our next appointment. We left Brasilia, to paraphrase Monty Python: 'for something completely different'.

CHAPTER 5

Phnom Penh: 1972–73

I WENT FROM BEING HEAD of Post, Brasilia to be Head of Chancery at the Embassy in Phnom Penh. As second-in command, the post was also what is now called 'Deputy Head of Mission'. Out of the eighteen months I was in Phnom Penh I was Chargé d'Affaires *ad interim* for a total of about six months. I was also Her Majesty's Consul, an additional role that, together with the dual role of political officer, personnel officer, and general manager of the Embassy for the ambassador, tempted me to describe myself as a modern Pooh-bah, Lord High Everything Else.

British policy regarding official files is that after thirty years they are opened to the public – with some exceptions where the material in the files is thought to be ultra-sensitive. In 2005 Jonathan Seager, a post-graduate student at Cambridge, wrote as his thesis: 'British Diplomatic Policy towards Cambodia 1965–1975'. I was delighted to discover that the very first paragraph of his Introduction to the subject began:

> In 1953 Winston Churchill remarked, 'I have lived seventy eight years without hearing of bloody places like Cambodia.' In a similar vein Richard Tallboys, Chargé d'Affaires in the British embassy Phnom Penh 1972–1973, recalled sometimes thinking, 'why are we [Britain] here?'

How nice to be quoted in the same paragraph as the great Winston Churchill. I do appear to be quoted by name in Jonathan's paper more often than any other individual. I suspect that not having the constraints instilled by the more traditional entry and career path in HM Diplomatic Service I was inclined to use more colourful phraseology than my colleagues.

Prior to French withdrawal from Vietnam in 1954 Britain did indeed have very little involvement or interest in Cambodia. But the end of French rule in Indochina was followed by Britain, with the Soviet Union, chairing the Geneva Conference on Indochina. For anyone interested in why we were there in 1972 I certainly recommend Jonathan Seager's paper.

My interest in Cambodia was more specific to the years 1972 and 1973. In recalling our experiences in those years I have continued to say that Phnom Penh was for Margaret and for me not only our most exciting post but also the saddest. I became accustomed to saying at the time that it was increasingly clear what the end was going to be. The question was how long would the agony continue.

In his thesis Jonathan Seager notes having found in the files a comment of mine, written in March 1973 during one of my spells as British Chargé d'Affaires: I had said in a message to South East Asia Department that I hoped my grim opinion was not being unduly influenced by having had several days without electricity. I had also written: 'The Khmer Republic staggers on from lurch to lurch, kept afloat for another week, just, on a sea of greenbacks.' – adding that 'the only optimists that Phnom Penh could now muster are of legendary Scots variety who are full of confidence that things can only indeed get worse, much worse.'

I did not foresee just how awful the end would be. Nor how good Cambodians whom we had got to know in the government of President Lon Nol, and who stayed on in the belief that some compromise could be arranged with the victors, would be slaughtered immediately the Khmer Rouge occupied Phnom Penh in 1975. I came increasingly to realise that the Americans were not the only people failing to understand the Vietnamese and Cambodians; what happened in 1975 showed that Cambodians did not understand other Cambodians.

I am an admirer of Gilbert and Sullivan, particularly of Gilbert's allusions to political and cultural attitudes. From time to time I see in a real present-day situation something that has a distinctly Gilbertian flavour to it, not necessarily a humorous one. A current worry agitating our American colleagues at the time Margaret and I arrived in Phnom Penh recalled for me something from *The Mikado*. One of the subjects of diplomatic discussion was the 'ghost voices' broadcasting on Free Khmer Radio. The 'ghosts' were Khieu Samphan and Hu Nin, both of whom had been condemned to death when Sihanouk was still in charge. Both of the men had been opponents of Sihanouk's rule, so it was of concern to the Americans and other Lon Nol supporters that the voices of two respected but believed dead dissidents should be broadcasting in support of the Khmer Rouge.

The US Embassy went to great lengths to try to convince everyone that the broadcast voices were not the real voices of the two individuals but were those of impersonators. Indeed on one occasion one of the US intelligence community called round to see me to show me photographs of Khieu Samphan that the 'opposition' were circulating, claiming that they had been taken recently on a rural highway. My visitor emphasised that the photos were clearly fakes as 'that stretch of roadway depicted in the background was under control of the Phnom Penh government forces at the date the photo was supposed to be have been taken'. I chose not to point out that even I could tell from the condition of the road surface and the growth at the edges of the road, that the roadway had clearly not had any traffic on it for a long time and I did not think that my visitor was correctly reading the Khmer numeral on the milestone in the picture. I fear it was one example of experiences that have over the years led to me to wonder about the intelligence of some 'intelligence' personnel.

The US view was that Khieu Samphan and Hu Nin had been condemned to death in Sihanouk's time, and that having been condemned they would then have been executed; after all there had then been no credible sighting of either man nor reports of any individuals with those names. Hence the popular broadcasters for the Khmer Free Radio had to be 'ghost voices'. I was tempted to say that the CIA should have studied *The Mikado*. In the Gilbert and Sullivan piece Nanki Poo, under the Mikado's law, had committed the capital offence of flirting. Having been convicted it was then considered by the characters in the story that Nanki Poo was as good as dead; and if he was as good as dead then there was no need to actually cut his head off. He could simply go and live elsewhere under another name. It seemed to me that that is what happened with Khieu Samphan and Hu Nin. Having been condemned to death the two men were as good as dead. Khieu Samphan and Hu Nin left the court by the proverbial 'side door' and disappeared into the jungle under different names, to resurface later under their own names as the embarrassing voices on Free Khmer Radio. Khieu Samphan and Hu Nin were indeed both very much alive in 1972. Hu Nin died in the 1980s, but more than thirty years after the Khmer Rouge took over the whole of Cambodia, Kheiu Samphan was alive and awaiting trial on 'war crimes'. Khieu Samphan's reputation was as an intelligent and honest critic of the Cambodian government of Sihanouk, and later that of General Lon Nol. I would be surprised if any war trial can show clear personal responsibility on Khieu Samphan's part for the horrors committed by the side he backed in opposition to Sihanouk and Lon Nol.

The siege of Phnom Penh got tighter as each dry season came round. It was almost a classic long-siege situation, one that endured for several years until eventually Phnom Penh became impossible to supply and hold. Each year the 'enemy' ring around Phnom Penh got closer to the edge of the city, with increasingly frequent 'fire-fights' taking place in the suburbs and in the vicinity of the airport. Within Phnom Penh there was debate as to whether incidents around the city and elsewhere were actually initiated by Vietnamese infiltrators rather than by the Cambodian insurgents on their own. Some thought that the Cambodians of the Khmer Rouge could not have been expert enough to do some of the damage without them having support from the North Vietnamese. The fraught relationship between the leaders of the Khmer Rouge and the Vietnamese was not fully appreciated until after the fighting was all over.

From time to time the situation in Phnom Penh would seem to be so desperate that occupation of the city was considered imminent. An instruction would come from London ordering the evacuation of all Embassy wives and children to Bangkok, leaving open for the time being the possibility of their return to Cambodia if the situation improved, as indeed it did from time to time.

The first evacuation of wives and children took place early in our stay. By the second and third evacuation families had got used to the procedure and took the process as routine. But the first evacuation was definitely stressful for the wives landing in Bangkok with children in tow. There was an unfortunate and surprising discovery when the wives disembarked from their aircraft and found that not one of the Bangkok Embassy wives, or a female member of Embassy staff, had come to the airport to meet them and help with the children. Such neglect was certainly not in the traditions of the Service, where care and assistance for colleagues' families was a high priority among members and their wives.

This lack of attention was upsetting for both the wives arriving in Bangkok and their husbands left in Phnom Penh. The wives were told that not one of the Bangkok Embassy wives was allowed to go to the airport to meet them because the wife of the Ambassador had insisted that she needed every Embassy wife to be present at her meeting being held that morning to plan a diplomatic tennis tournament. On the principle taught to me by my parents that 'to know all is to forgive all', it would not surprise me if Lady Delamare was such a strong personality that no junior member of the Embassy was brave enough to argue with her to emphasise the effect on morale of the evacuees if not a single Embassy wife was at the airport to welcome them.

During one evacuation in late 1972 my wife and children were placed by the Bangkok Embassy in a hotel that turned out to be more or less a brothel for American troops on R and R. Margaret took the children to where she thought they might get a soft drink. Upon entering what appeared to be the hotel lounge she was surprised how dark the room was. As the family entered the lounge the lights were turned up and Margaret realised that the room was occupied by young men and women, most of whom were in close contact with each other. Margaret and the children left quickly and the lights were turned down again. Upon hearing of the experience I made a fuss and obtained agreement that the family could move to a hotel at the beach resort of Pattaya. In some ways the hotel at Pattaya wasn't much better, but at least there was a beach and a baby elephant to keep the children amused until they went back to school at the beginning of the next school term in England. Margaret then rejoined me in Phnom Penh. There were no such mishaps in late July 1973 when wives and non-essential staff were again evacuated to Bangkok. On that occasion Margaret's evacuation was final.

In between the 'scares', life in Phnom Penh seemed safe, safe enough at least for our children to come for the school holidays. In 1972 Margaret's mother 'Bobbie' Strutt came for a week or so while the children were with us. Bobbie had her own adventure. She had taken the nine-year-old twins Peter and Sarah for a visit to the Central Market. They were just leaving the market when all hell broke loose. Hand grenades were going off accompanied by a fusillade of automatic rifle fire. Bobbie's reaction was to move with the crowd fleeing away from the action but young Peter was much more interested in going in the opposite direction to see what the excitement was about. Bobbie managed to get him to stop just as a Cambodian pharmacist, who was in the process of quickly bringing down the metal shutter on his shop entrance, grabbed all three of them and hauled them into his shop as the shutter banged shut. It was not until five hours later that we could send the Embassy driver back to the market area to collect the family. On her return home to Hobart Bobbie dined off that story for quite some time.

Margaret and I must have spent hundreds of hours on our balcony watching the war activity of one form or another. When at night we were woken up by the noise of explosions or by the house shaking, we could never at first be sure whether we had been woken by a B52 bomber dropping its load fifteen miles out of Phnom Penh, or whether the gunfire was the beginning of another incursion into the city itself. Some of those incursions were quite serious, especially one that took place in the vicinity of the French Embassy in 1972.

Many years later, looking through the letters that her mother had collected, Margaret came across one that she had written to her mother in November 1972, not long after Bobbie's visit to us in Phnom Penh. It described a typical evening:

> We woke at 2.30 a.m. when the air conditioner stopped and we heard rockets, mortars and machine guns. We flew to the corner where you used to take shelter and sat low until we had some idea of what was going on. The Viets came in on motor bikes, got on the unimportant bridge (across the Mekong); the one that goes to the navy headquarters – the road goes nowhere else. Dressed as a pregnant woman, explosives all around her, she, with her 'husband' was allowed across. The guard went back to sleep. They stopped in the middle, slid over the side, laid explosives well down, got back up on to the bridge and drove away. One span of the bridge was blasted into the river to stop river traffic etc. So now we have just the one bridge and the airport (as exit routes).
>
> Sappers also got in, captured five tanks on army property and drove like mad to get away, but all were killed. The bodies were then put by the river, plus a tank, for three days. Bodies are popular (as a sight) but hardly a soul viewed the tank.
>
> The Royal or Le Phnom Hotel had rockets fired nearby. A new member of staff and his wife were in the hotel and heard the lot, including a drunken soldier firing his gun in the air. All the hotel guests tried to find cover in the hall of the hotel and when we telephoned, the porter assured us that 'all was well'. Then one man thought he saw a Vietcong behind the French Embassy, so they all shot thru' the front of the embassy, wrecking walls, chairs, typewriters etc. We went back to sleep at about 5 a.m. – but the fighting went on until 9 a.m.

One can become blasé about the most unpleasant disturbances and not lose too much sleep if such things happen repeatedly. The night that Margaret wrote about was just another of many such nights.

Our time in Cambodia coincided with the American B52 bombing in the country. The bombing was the Nixon Administration's 'illegal' bombing of Cambodia that caused so much of a problem for the US

Administration when it became public knowledge. When each flight of bombers released its load the sight of the red flashes across the horizon, followed a few seconds later by the noise and the shock wave, was frightening enough when it was fifteen miles away. One can only try to imagine what it must have been like for the Cambodian peasants living in the countryside much closer to the explosions.

In his paper on British Diplomatic Policy towards Cambodia, Jonathan Seager notes under a heading 'Congressional limitations on US activity in Cambodia', that:

> The US embassy had extended its role beyond what it had been sanctioned to do. James Lowenstein, who had been sent by the Senate Foreign Relations Committee to Cambodia to investigate US activity, later recalled finding out about the embassy's role through accidentally hearing American air controllers directing planes on a local radio frequency.

On one occasion we were woken by the shaking of the house and went out on to our bedroom balcony to see what might be going on. Was it just more B52 bombing fifteen or more miles out of Phnom Penh or was it the beginning of a final attack on the city? We stood together looking out towards the city boundaries, but all was quiet. It was a perfectly clear moonlit night with the full moon high above us.

I chanced to look up at the moon and witnessed the extraordinary sight of a flight of three B52 bombers silhouetted against the face of the full moon. The image occurred to me later as being of three witches on broomsticks returning from their evil deed of the night. By the time I had got Margaret's attention to look upwards to the moon the planes were already half way out of the moon's orb. It turned out that what we had seen was the flight of B52 bombers that instead of dropping their bombs on an 'enemy' location had, owing to a faulty navigation beacon, dropped their load on the government-held town of Neak Loong a few miles down river from the capital. The devastation and casualties of that bombing error was re-created as the opening scenes of the film *The Killing Fields*, a film that in its early sequences also recreates with disturbing reality the atmosphere of Phnom Penh towards the end of my time there.

The reaction when the bombing campaign was discovered led to some interesting situations as a result of Congress decreeing that only two hundred American 'officials' should be in Cambodia at any one time. This meant, for example, that when General Alexander Haig flew in with an entourage, the American Embassy were expected to fly a group of their people out to Saigon to keep the total official personnel present down to two hundred during the Haig visit. As I was Chargé at the time of the Haig visit I got an invitation to the lunch for him. It is always interesting, though not always reassuring, to see in the flesh people who are prominent in the media.

One of the more spectacular night-time sights was the occasional view of 'Puff the Magic Dragon' firing on the outskirts of Phnom Penh. 'Puff' was a DC3 with a fixed multiple-barrel rapid-fire gun fitted amidships and pointing out through a door in the side of the aircraft. The DC3 would fly quite low in a slow circular orbit around the target on the ground, thus concentrating its tremendous fire-power on a small area without having to actually sight the weapon itself. This was at that time a fairly safe operation for the aircraft as it was before the advent of the SAM missiles such as were later used in Afghanistan. The Khmer Rouge and Viet Cong had no anti-aircraft weapons. From four or five miles distance the fireworks display from sky to ground was spectacular. What it was like for any humans in the target area did not bear thinking about.

There was no question but that Margaret's mother's experience in the Central Market of Phnom Penh, when she and the twins were rescued by a Cambodian pharmacist dragging them into his shop and sheltering them from the mayhem outside, was an incident created by a Cambodian soldier who had for some reason run amok, just as later the only British casualty in Cambodia was a victim of a police colonel who had done the same in a bar. However, from time to time there were reports of incidents such as hand-grenades being rolled down the aisles of local cinemas, or thrown into the last two restaurants catering for Europeans. Such incidents were always blamed on Khmer Rouge or Vietnamese 'terrorists' seeking to disrupt ordinary life in the city. I personally have not the slightest doubt they were in reality eruptions from protection rackets being conducted by locals, either military or police controlled. Similarly the attempt to blow up the US Deputy Head of Mission, Tom Enders, was I am sure an attempt by elements of the Cambodian military who felt they weren't getting enough kickbacks from the US material and financial support of their army.

The Cambodian army was a force of doubtful value in attempts to defeat either the Khmer Rouge or such Vietnamese allies as the Khmer Rouge may have had in the rural areas. The concept of an imported political ideology such as communism would have meant nothing to rural or uneducated city Khmer, any more than the concept or value of democracy would mean anything to them. For most ordinary Cambodians, their sense of loyalty had always been first to their King, and then perhaps to their fellow Cambodians' struggle against encroaching Thais from the west and encroaching Vietnamese from the east. The idea of risking their lives for some political idea or for a government led by an army general would not have induced in them any great military sense of a duty to fight.

Many believed that the Cambodian situation would have been very different politically as well as militarily if Sirik Matak had been leader of the country instead of either Sihanouk or later Lon Nol. He was a tough character whose branch of the country's royal family could have given him a claim to the throne and might have given the country a leader the rural population would have seen as their legitimate leader as compared to Lon Nol.

I have a vivid memory of an evening at Sirik Matak's house. I was seated at one end of a settee with the Prime Minister, In Tam, sitting at the other end. General John Cleland who headed the Military Equipment Development Commission was seated between us. The General was a likable man to know personally and a typical enthusiastic and dedicated United States officer. His character and style in fulfilling his role in the 'war effort' led me to refer to him in a communication to London as 'General John Praise the Lord and Pass the Ammunition Cleland'. He was doing his utmost to inspire and enthuse the Cambodian military to make good use of all the equipment and ammunition he was delivering to them.

On this informal evening occasion General Cleland was being emphatic in telling the Prime Minister about the need for the Cambodian army to get more troops out on the south-west outskirts of Phnom Penh and, to quote him, 'hit them hard'. As the General emphasised his point, leaning forward with gestures, I looked across his back to In Tam at the other end of the settee. The Prime Minister was in his turn looking at me and raising his eyebrows in a manner which I took as much as to mean: 'Don't the Americans understand that young Cambodians didn't join their army to fight and "hit them hard"; they joined as officers because they expected to make some money on the side; or as private soldiers because then they at least had food and clothing.'

The Deputy Head of Mission at the United States Embassy was Tom Enders. Tom was for the whole of my time in Phnom Penh the key person in relations between the US Embassy and the local military. Tom was well over six feet tall and indeed a handsome man. He looked much more like the general image of a tough American general than General Cleland or General Haig. Tom's wife Gaetana was certainly the grandest hostess in town and no one would want to miss one of her parties. Sadly for our social life Gaetana did not spend that much of her time in Phnom Penh.

Tom Enders had been installed as DHM in 1971 at the insistence of the White House rather than the US State Department. The Kissinger faction apparently wanted someone more gung-ho on site, someone who would be more supportive of the US military activity in Cambodia and not too worried that such activity might have been specifically forbidden by Congress. In Cambodia the military support was direct and on a dramatic and deadly scale, including as it did not just the supply of military weaponry but also the period of B52 bombing and the use of aircraft such as F111s; aircraft that were certainly beyond the capability of the Cambodian air force.

The way in which Tom Enders carried out his role as US Deputy Head of Mission did not make him universally popular, even with all of the people he was trying to help. By chance I witnessed the attempt to assassinate him. I woke earlier than usual one morning. To avoid disturbing Margaret I left our bedroom to walk across the first-floor landing to make use of the guest bathroom. The landing had open grills instead of windows. As I walked across there was a loud bang and a hundred yards or so away a huge plume of black smoke rose beyond the trees of the neighbouring garden. It was the attempt to blow Tom up. His car was badly damaged but Tom simply got out of the vehicle and walked away unharmed. The bomb, planted in a food cart at the side of the road, had been so inefficiently placed that the strength of the explosion went upwards into the air instead of into the Embassy car. If the Khmer Rouge or Viet Cong had been responsible I have no doubt the explosion would not have been so ineffective. I suspect the assassination attempt was just as likely to have been the action of a group of Cambodians who felt Tom was not managing the support in a way to their liking, for which read 'hadn't put enough money in their direction'.

The US Ambassador was Coby Swank, a fine career diplomat who tried very hard to have his Embassy work according to the rules laid down by Congress. This did not make him popular with those who saw their future advancement as coming through their support for Kissinger's attitudes to Vietnam, rather than adhering to the policies and actions that Congress and the State Department wished to pursue.

The war in the countryside led to the population of the Phnom Penh city area increasing from about 250,000 to nearly 1 million as more and more rural peasants took refuge in the city. The peasants were undoubtedly seeking shelter as much from the bombing as from the Khmer Rouge. By the time I left every pagoda compound had filled with refugees and their bullock carts. It became harder and harder for the Americans to maintain supplies. Convoys of supply ships would be heavily attacked during each dry season when the navigable channel of the Mekong was narrow. At such times attackers could simply wait for the ships to come past close to their hiding places dug into the banks of the river. During the wet season, when the river was full and the channel much wider, supplies were easier as the convoys did not have to adhere to one narrow channel. Each year the supply situation became a little more difficult.

There was also present in Phnom Penh a group of five or six British ex-service supply officers. These were 'Third Country Nationals' working in the logistics system that the Americans had built up to supply the Cambodian military with equipment and ammunition: MEDC, the Military Equipment Development Commission headed by General John Cleland. The British members of the US-financed team, along with a much larger number of Koreans and Filipinos, being 'TCNs' did not count towards the legitimate two hundred US official personnel allowed to be in the country at any one time. They were, furthermore, ostensibly all in Cambodia as civilians. It just happened that in addition to the British members of the team all the Koreans and Filipinos were retired colonels from their own military.

In the 1970s the Royal Air Force maintained an executive aircraft in Bangkok for the use of British diplomatic missions in the region as a means of travel to the more outlying parts. The plane spent six months in Bangkok, if I remember correctly, and various periods in Jakarta, Vientiane and so on. For some time each year the plane went to Rangoon and was available to Phnom Penh for a week. When Phnom Penh's turn came round in 1973 I was Chargé. So for one week I had at my disposal my own RAF twin-engine turbo-prop executive aircraft to take me, the Defence Attaché and another member of staff to places that certainly none of my non-American diplomatic colleagues were able to visit and which few foreigners of any kind would visit for a very long time to come. Siem Reap, Kompong Cham, Kompong Chnang, Battambang, and the port of

Sihanoukville were all visited. I took every advantage to see as much as possible of the country.

My only view of Angkor Wat was through a mist, with the well-known outline silhouetted in the distance. We could not get closer to the ruins because they were occupied by the Khmer Rouge. The Siem Reap airport was within mortar range of Angkor Wat, so our plane could not land there. The Cambodians were certainly not keen on any suggestions of trying to drive the Khmer Rouge out of the ancient site, though it was rumoured that the Americans were considering bombing it. Instead of landing at the Siem Reap airport my 'personal executive aircraft' provided by the RAF landed on a strip of roadway that had been widened by clearing the jungle for a few metres on either side and widening the dirt road itself sufficiently to enable DC3s such as those of Air America to land and replenish the local garrison.

In widening the airstrip a small temple ruin had been uncovered from where it had been completely hidden in a massive bamboo thicket. While Angkor Wat might have been inaccessible, a team of archeologists was, in the middle of the fighting, still working on clearing the site of the recent discovery. With a military escort we had the opportunity to inspect a miniature version of the great temples that were out of reach to any visitors at the time.

The only item that I recall relating to the advancement of British exports was the receipt of a large and colourful poster promoting high performance British motorcars. I decided it would brighten up our working environment if we hung the bright and optimistic poster from London on the wall of the reception area. That poster was the clue to me knowing that the author John Le Carré must have visited Cambodia soon after my departure. The poster received a mention in his novel *The Honourable Schoolboy*. I was the diplomat who thought we should put up the poster to brighten things up when we were at the same time in the process of building sand-bag walls around the ground-floor windows and planning an 'evacuation rehearsal'. I recommend that one chapter of Le Carré's book as being a worthwhile independent description, fiction as it is, of what it was like in Phnom Penh in the final weeks before I left Cambodia at the end of 1973. Several of the fictional incidents in the chapter echo some of the real experiences I had, though there is a considerable amount of novelist's licence and exaggeration in the detail and the timing. Le Carré's novel refers, for example, to a disgruntled Cambodian pilot dropping a bomb on the presidential palace. That did actually happen but it was in March 1973, not at the time of the fictional visit.

In the deteriorating situation in Cambodia the 'Office' decided that instead of sending our children out to Phnom Penh for the July 1973 school holidays, my wife should instead return to London. I stayed on until December 1973. Certainly, by the time I left the situation was becoming very nasty. I have a recollection of having afternoon tea on our upper terrace with a visiting BBC executive. As we enjoyed our tea we had my field glasses handy and were able to watch aircraft dive-bombing not far away. We were close enough so that with the glasses we could see the bombs leave an aircraft and drop behind the trees. Fortunately for our sense of relaxation, we knew that between us and whoever it was that was being bombed, there was the Mekong River.

So what were we at the British Embassy doing there? I am sure the answer is that the British Embassy was there almost solely so that we could be seen to be supporting the American position of recognising the government of General Lon Nol. There was indeed a good political argument for having a Western European diplomatic presence in Cambodia at a time when the 'domino' theory of Communist penetration of the whole of South East Asia was still current. Several other Western countries had a diplomatic presence in Phnom Penh. The Germans and Japanese each had only a permanent Chargé d'Affaires, but the French had a large embassy, as one might expect in one of their ex-colonial territories, and the Australians maintained a significant embassy establishment. The real purpose was clearly to support and be seen to support the American position defending Cambodia against the 'Communists', rather than for any real British interest in Cambodia itself.

On my last Sunday in Cambodia I accepted an invitation from a Jamaican 'student' to ride on the back of his motorcycle to see the scene of a 'fire-fight' that had taken place just beyond the airport boundary the night before. Just what the 'student', his delightful wife and their two pretty little daughters were doing in Phnom Penh I don't know and didn't ask. He was a pleasant and well-informed acquaintance.

The Sunday excursion proved to be an alarming and nasty experience. Just past the airport we realised we were close to the battle zone when we came across a line of some twenty very mangled bodies laid out on the verge beside the road. We stopped to inspect the grisly scene and from what I saw beside the road that Sunday I certainly came to appreciate just how fragile the human body is. The grisliest television CSI stories do not match the real thing. When we asked a soldier how far away the enemy were he pointed out clumps of trees two or three hundred yards away where the remnants of the Khmer Rouge band were believed to be hiding. We decided it was time to return to safer ground. I also realised then that perhaps the FCO had been right in insisting that Phnom Penh was no longer a place for our children to spend their school holidays.

Towards the close of my tour of duty in Cambodia, during my last period as Chargé, a farewell dinner was held in my honour at Le Phnom. What had once been the top hotel in the city was by then an almost empty mouldering pile. It wasn't a large dinner party but it was very kind of Prime Minister In Tam and Foreign Minister Long Boret to take the time and trouble to arrange the dinner and to attend. There were more important concerns for them to attend to as the situation for the Lon Nol government became increasingly desperate. During the course of the evening both In Tam and Long Boret told me of their regret about Cambodia's plight and said of the coup against the then government supporting Sihanouk: 'It was a mistake. It wasn't meant that the King should stay away permanently. It was intended as a warning to him.' All I could think of their comment was that it was 'Too late now.'

CHAPTER 6

A consular duty to be done

IN 1972 AND 1973 I WAS HEAD of Chancery and what would today be called – in the American style – Deputy Head of Mission at the Embassy in Phnom Penh. I had the additional title and responsibilities as Her Majesty's Consul. My Commission as Consul bore Her Majesty's signature and indicated that my responsibilities in that role were:

> . . . to take care of the affairs of Our said Subjects, and to aid and assist them in all their lawful and mercantile concerns [and] by all lawful means to aid and protect Our Merchants and others Our Subjects who may trade with or visit or reside within his Consular District . . .

It is always pleasant to receive documents bearing Her Majesty's 'sign manual' but it does not mean that all such diplomatic formalities are executed promptly. It was only while writing this memoir that I realised that the Commission as Consul is dated 'Tenth of June 1973' by which time I had been in Phnom Penh almost a year and was beginning to think of leaving.

The 'British Community' in Phnom Penh in 1972 and 1973 was very small indeed; so my consular duties were minimal. The Second Secretary, Frank Callaghan, doubled as Vice Consul and was available to attend to routine consular matters if and when any such matters arose. He also doubled as the Commercial Officer and whatever. More relevant to community morale was that Frank and his wife provided the venue for the annual Burns Night Supper, for which the haggis was flown out with the compliments of British Airways: definitely a more exotic location than usual for a Burns Night Supper. About twenty people, including three or four genuine Scots, gathered in a back room at the Vice-Consul's house with limited lighting and occasional 'noises off' from the bombing in the background.

Apart from Embassy personnel the British community included the Chartered Bank manager and his wife, a journalist from Reuters more or less permanently resident at the Phnom Hotel, and a rather unusual responsibility in the form of a Jamaican 'student'. My official interest in him was that as a Commonwealth citizen he was on my list of those to be borne in mind in times of crisis. There was also present in Phnom Penh a British Council representative running an English language school; but I cannot recall any others apart from the group of five who were, as Third Country Nationals, assisting the Americans in their logistical problems of supplying military equipment and ammunition to the Cambodian army.

The siege of Phnom Penh got tighter as each dry season passed. It was becoming increasingly likely that at any time we might have to initiate a warning to the British community regarding their safety. The warning had three phases. The first would be to warn members of the community that they and their families should leave Cambodia unless their presence was essential. The second phase would be to warn the community that they should all leave the country as soon as possible. The third phase would be to advise that all members of the British community should proceed to the British Embassy in preparation for protection and earliest possible evacuation. In practical terms the final message meant that in a final collapse of Phnom Penh we would almost certainly need to rely on our American friends to get our small community out of the country. Whichever of the 'warning' messages needed to be sent it would require a written letter to be delivered to each of the addresses that we had recorded for those Commonwealth citizens who were not specifically the responsibility of the Australian Embassy.

Events were moving very quickly in Cambodia and the need for an instant warning could arise at any time. There would be little time for the small Embassy staff to sit down and produce the necessary letter, have it addressed and get it delivered around the city. So I prepared letters for each stage and, having had them addressed to the individuals we knew of I had the three bundles of letters placed in the secure strongroom. The prepared letters were under strict rules of confidentiality so that the word did not get about that the Embassy might be getting nervous. In my time we had just one occasion in which to send out the first of the three letters and were able to have them on their way from the Embassy within minutes of the decision that a warning was warranted.

My consular responsibilities did provide me with one adventure that had the flavour of a movie such as *The Third Man* or *Casablanca*. This involved a British citizen whom we did not expect to have to worry about as far as welfare and possible evacuation was concerned. He was one of the small group of retired British military supply officers working in Cambodia on contract with the Americans.

My consular adventure came late on an evening when Margaret and I had been at the Ambassador's residence for dinner. I was driving the Embassy Land-Rover back to our house at about midnight, well after the 10 p.m. curfew. As in other countries, diplomats in Phnom Penh were not subject to the restrictions of a curfew. At that hour of the night well into the curfew there was, not surprisingly, no other traffic. The city had very limited street lighting, indeed very little lighting of any kind, something that served to enhance the effect of the 'fireworks' to be seen in the distance around the outskirts of the city. I drove carefully down the middle of the wide and almost completely darkened boulevard leading towards the Embassy Chancery building. The cautious driving was not because I was concerned at the possibility of a Khmer Rouge or Vietcong attack on us. The caution was for fear that if we travelled fast and noisily we might wake up some sleeping Cambodian guard whose immediate reaction would be to fire his automatic weapon in panic at whatever might be in front of him.

Arriving at our house, a modest but agreeable French villa adjacent to the Embassy Chancery, I parked the Land-Rover at the kerb. As Margaret and I approached the front door I could hear the telephone ringing. When I picked up the phone from the hall table the caller proved to be from the Consular Department of the US Embassy. His brief advice was that 'One of your people has caught it.' He went on to explain that one of the five or six British personnel working as TCNs had been shot dead when caught up in an incident in a bar earlier in the evening. My caller then added the information that the body of the unfortunate man was still lying at the bar on a main street in the city.

It transpired that a Cambodian police colonel, not at the time wearing uniform, had been evicted from the bar earlier in the day. Some hours later the victim of the shooting, whom I shall refer to as 'Charlie', though that was not his real name, had at the end of his day's work been having a quiet beer by himself at a table in the same bar. Those customers present at the earlier time, having seen the argument between the bar management and the police colonel, were aware that it would not be surprising if the offended Cambodian policeman were to return later and cause trouble. So all the earlier customers had discreetly gone elsewhere while the new patrons such as Charlie, being unaware of the earlier fuss, had no suspicion that something might go wrong. The police colonel returned to the bar, in full uniform, and upon entering simply sprayed the whole interior with a fusillade of bullets. Charlie, sitting quietly at a table by himself, was hit in the back of the neck by a ricochet from the ceiling. The ricochet killed him instantly. He was the only fatality. Not surprisingly everyone else in the bar disappeared quickly. No one had told Charlie or the other customers about the incident earlier in the day.

My immediate problem was to decide what I, as Her Majesty's Consul, should do about the body of the unfortunate British subject. I could of course have telephoned the Vice Consul and passed the problem to him but that did not seem the decent thing to do in the circumstances of Phnom Penh. I at least had a rough idea of the location of the bar where I was told I could expect to find the body. But I did not speak Khmer and my French would almost certainly have not been much use trying to interrogate the Cambodians in the area immediately around the bar, even if any of them were prepared to appear to talk to a single European turning up on his own at one o'clock in the morning when all Cambodians were supposed to be at home and in bed. There were no municipal 'emergency' services I could call upon, nor any other Cambodian authorities I could expect to telephone successfully in the middle of the night. I came to the conclusion that the problem was mine.

Fortunately I knew who Charlie worked for and where his boss lived. So I set off by myself in the Land-Rover to drive across the dark curfewed city with intermittent fireworks bursting in the distance. At least there was no traffic along my route. Once on the far side of the city I turned off the sealed road and along a dirt track through what in the headlights had all the appearance of jungle but was in reality a relatively new up-market suburb for middle class Cambodians.

The TCNs, of which the deceased Charlie was one, were headed by a British individual who lived with his wife in a nice two-storey house in a suburb that had middle-class residences although the roads in the area were not sealed. For the purpose of this account I shall call him 'Reggie'. Reggie and his wife were a couple I not only liked but for whom I had respect. They were also good hosts. Reggie never gossiped about what he was doing and I didn't ask. But I did know that the TCNs were a device by which the US Executive under President Johnson got around the Congressional ruling that there could be no more than two hundred American officials in Cambodia at any one time.

Although the TCNs were not – at least not as far as I know – doing any fighting they were there to provide the logistic support necessary to get to the Cambodian military the arms and ammunition being shipped in by the

USA to keep the Lon Nol army in business. Apart from my friend Reggie, who headed the operation, there were five or six retired British supply officers and below them a large team of a hundred or more Koreans and Filipinos. All of the latter were of course also in Cambodia as civilians. It was no more than coincidence that all these civilians just happened to be retired officers from their own respective military forces. This TCN activity in Cambodia did not as far as I know attract any attention from the US Congress. I cannot recall seeing any reference to TCNs in the media or indeed in official British correspondence. There was apparently no mention of it in the Foreign Office files that were opened for public inspection in 2005.

I arrived at the house of Charlie's 'leader' having driven alone through the darkened and deserted streets from one side of Phnom Penh to the other, with the sounds and flashes of incidents on the outskirts adding to the rather weird atmosphere of my journey. I pressed the bell button on the closed iron gates only to be greeted by the Cambodian housekeeper who made it clear to me that the man I was looking for was not at home.

I sat in the Land-Rover for some minutes wondering just what I might do next. At the very least I would have to drive back to the centre of the city on my own and make some attempt to find out what had happened to Charlie's body. Just as I was about to set off once more on my solitary search, the man I was hoping to meet drove up in a veritable convoy of Jeeps packed with armed Cambodian soldiers as his bodyguard.

I explained what had happened to one of his team and then joined his convoy as it reversed direction and we set off for the city bar. If the large escort Reggie had with him indicated the level of risk he personally was exposed to, I did wonder whether I might not actually have been safer driving alone. On arriving in the darkened street location of the bar where Charlie's body was supposed to be, the noise and lights of the convoy attracted some locals to come out on their apartment balconies. A dialogue between the Cambodian escort and the residents disclosed that the body had been taken to the Phnom Penh public hospital. The convoy set off again. By this time it was about 2 a.m.

At the hospital entrance there was hardly any lighting, but as we drove through the entrance of the hospital compound casualties of the war appeared from the surrounding shadows to stand silently around to see what the activity was about. All had varying quantities of dirty bandages around various parts of their bodies; some were on crutches and others had clearly lost limbs. It was a scene out of some particularly unpleasant horror film.

The mortuary was pointed out to us. Reggie and I walked over to the few steps leading up to the mortuary entrance doorway. Over the steps was a single light bulb providing just enough light for me to see large dark, slightly shiny stains on the steps. It did not need much imagination to realise we were stepping over bloodstains. Opening the door of the mortuary we were faced with a veritable charnel house. Bodies were lying on wooden racks as well as all over the floor of a large area, each roughly wrapped in grubby stained white sheets. There must have been at least a hundred bodies of recent casualties. It was however easy to identify in the middle of the group of more recent arrivals the one European corpse, lying stretched out on the floor in the middle of the mortuary.

The public hospital mortuary had no air-conditioning, let alone any refrigeration operating. The atmosphere was definitely unpleasant. It was decided that we couldn't leave Charlie where he was; so my companion got his guards to bully an ambulance driver, who appeared to be drunk, to load up the body and accompany our convoy to the French hospital, where it was assumed conditions would be better. The conditions at the 'best' hospital in Phnom Penh were better but not much. There weren't as many bodies and there was a rather ineffective air-conditioner rattling away. We left Charlie there and Reggie said he would organise a funeral.

Two or three days later I gathered with Reggie and some of the other British TCNs at the local cemetery. Also present were a number of Cambodian officials and military officers, together with sheepish-looking representatives of the police force, one of whose senior officers had been responsible for Charlie's death. It was a gloomy rainy day with rain dripping off the surrounding tall trees as we stood around the open grave. The burial site was surrounded by colonial-era gravestones on two of which I could read that they marked the last resting places of officers of the French Foreign Legion. I recall the impression that the scene was a cross between *The Third Man* and *Casablanca*.

Charlie's next of kin had to be informed of his death. It was my task as Consul to write and explain what had happened and the arrangements for the burial. I received a reply from Charlie's sister. Her letter expressed appreciation for what had been done. The letter went on to say that she and their mother were saddened but they knew that Charlie was very happy with what he was doing in Cambodia. His work was close to what he had been doing throughout his career before retirement. His sister explained that there was nothing for him to be involved with at home; he had no family other than her and their very elderly mother. The sister's letter ended by saying they were content that Charlie had died happy doing something he was enjoying and that they were grateful for the arrangements made for him to be buried in Phnom Penh. That was perhaps as 'happy' an ending as one might wish for in response to a Consul's unfortunate duty.

I left Cambodia while Reggie and the TCNs were still actively involved in efforts to bolster the increasingly demoralised Cambodian government army. Margaret and I went once more for dinner at the house along the unmade road through the suburb in the jungle. We have as a memento of that acquaintanceship a small Buddha figure given to us by Reggie and his wife as a parting gift. The last I heard of Reggie was that when the TCNs had to pack up and leave Cambodia he went off to Saudi Arabia to do something else for the US military. I do wonder whether the couple ever did manage to retire to the fourteenth century farmhouse they had bought in southern Portugal.

CHAPTER 7

London: 1974–76

A T THE END OF 1973 I RETURNED to the Foreign and Commonwealth Office in London to be Assistant Head of Department. I must have been doing something correctly in my previous posts as pleasant news arrived not long after we had left Phnom Penh. It came as a complete surprise when an impressive envelope landed on our front door-mat with the contents telling me that it was being considered recommending me for appointment as an Officer in the Most Excellent Order of the British Empire. If I was to be so recommended would I accept? Needless to say I replied positively.

My first job on this second spell in London was as Assistant Head of Gibraltar and General Department at the Foreign and Commonwealth Office. The title of the department with its vague reference to 'General' made people think there must have been something mysterious and perhaps 'hush hush' about its activities. In fact it was all rather routine. G & G was a useful bin into which to drop tasks that didn't quite fit in to any of the geographical departments, each of which dealt with specific regions of the world.

G & G did deal with Gibraltar, though much of the management of that colony was in the hands of the Department of Defence. Otherwise G & G dealt with a range of matters concerning the small remnants of Empire. There was some useful application of my accounting experience in that I dealt with one or two proposals for legislation by Caribbean islands anxious to achieve tax-haven status as a way to earn income and attract funds. HM Treasury did not like such ideas, especially having noticed the success for the early venture into that field by the Cayman Islands; but the FCO interest, at least as far as I saw it, was to encourage anything that might make islands such as the British Virgin Islands less financially dependent on London.

For a couple of years I was Secretary to the Selection Board that put forward names of individuals for appointment as Governor to one of the few remaining Dependent Territories. 'Dependent Territories' had become the politically correct term for what were in effect still colonies. Dependent

Territories were distinct from Associated States, the latter being those 'colonies' that had moved on to taking more responsibility for their own affairs, a status that meant that at least they chose their own Governors and were places to which Britain sent High Commissioners. Observing the process for selection of Governors taught me that while appointment as Governor of Turks and Caicos Islands, or Governor of St Helena, might sound a prestigious and perhaps even rather glamorous position to hold, the jobs as Governor in such places gave me the distinct impression of being dead ends and perhaps rather boring. Jobs as Governor were however useful slots in to which could be fitted long-serving members of the Colonial Service for their final appointment before retirement.

Each of the territories published an Annual Report to the FCO and I found them rather dull reading. Especially dull appeared to be the report from the Falkland Islands. For one year the only picture the administration of the islands could find as an illustration of their annual activities was nothing more exciting than a photograph of the Governor, in uniform complete with plumed hat, getting out of a battered London taxi to inspect a group of bedraggled Boy Scouts. I concluded that nothing of interest ever happened in the Falklands. I wasn't always on the mark in my assessments!

In the 1970s the Foreign and Commonwealth Office was doing all it could subtly do to encourage Falkland islanders to see the long-term future for their children and grandchildren as being with a connection to Argentina. A direct flight to the mainland was subsidised; children were sent to English-speaking high schools in Argentina; and a resident teacher of Spanish was installed on the island – a person later to be recognised as probably having been something of a 'spy' for the Argentine military. The Argentine generals 'blew it' when they invaded the islands, thus ensuring that the Argentine cause has been set back for many years to come, probably for several generations as far as the Falkland Islanders themselves are concerned. By the beginning of the twenty-first century the Falklands were no longer a burden on the British taxpayer, not because of the rumoured offshore oil but because of the realisation of the money to be made from granting licences to fish in the Falklands 'economic zone' extending for two hundred miles all around the islands. I have quite recently visited the islands. On a sunny day they are pleasant and clearly not impoverished, but the countryside is spoilt by signs warning about land mines. The visit confirmed my early impression that the islands have distinct similarities to the Shetland Isles.

While the Falkland Islands were in 1974 and 1975 little more than a nuisance to the Foreign and Commonwealth Office, the islands were the very justification for the commercial existence of the Falkland Islands Company Ltd. The company was very effective in its lobbying activities with Parliament. It was not for nothing that the company had a prominent presence in the immediate vicinity of Whitehall. I later wondered what part that lobbying might have played in the matter of the Falkland Islands 'war' and the British reaction to the invasion. I certainly believe that the Argentine generals could have got away with it if the government of the day in Britain, whether Conservative or Labour, had been led by any Prime Minister other than Margaret Thatcher.

Gibraltar and General Department attended to 'labour' issues for the dependent territories. This subject was particularly related to the trade union influence in Gibraltar itself. I attended one session of the International Labour Organisation in Geneva, an experience that convinced me that the environment of such international conferences was definitely not for me; though I can well appreciate how living in an attractive city on a good salary and a job that expands to fill the time available, can offer an attractive life-style for many.

The Governor of Gibraltar was and has always been an appointment for a distinguished military officer, though the impression in 1974 was that the 'Rock' was in practical terms, with a Labour government in London, being run by and for the benefit of the local branch of the British Transport and General Workers Union. TGWU had all the shipyard workers as members and wielded considerable influence within the UK trade union movement and thus with the Labour Party, especially when the Labour Party formed the government in London. For many years the TGWU exerted particular influence because the shipyard was a key maintenance and repair facility for the Royal Navy. When the Gibraltar dockyards were later privatised a certain sense of reality struck the workforce.

Apart from the visit to the ILO in Geneva my only other official overseas travel while in G & G was to Gibraltar itself. This was at a time when almost a whole generation of Gibraltarians had grown up without ever being able to cross the causeway into Spain. Most of the population, with modest incomes from shipyard and public service jobs, lived in cramped municipal-style housing. Few Gibraltarians could afford to fly out of the island very often and although every family seemed to own a motor-car there were only three or four miles of road on the island. In reality it appeared that the family motor-car sat in the street to provide an additional family room where teenagers could gather away from their parents.

The UK's difficult relations with Spain over Spanish claims for the return of Gibraltar meant that one had to fly directly from London to Gibraltar without making a stop in Spain. So on the way out from London I could not stop over in Madrid to discuss the Gibraltar issues with staff of the Embassy there. The Spaniards would not allow visitors to enter Gibraltar from Spain. But only Hispanic logic would then raise no objection to me flying with British Airways directly from Gibraltar to Madrid on the way home. One day of meetings at the Embassy and a weekend as a back-packer tourist to Segovia and to Toledo suited me well.

A most interesting and enlightening task of my time with G & G Department was being Chairman of the Selection Board choosing young people for the last of the *Boy's Own Paper* type of colonial job. In 1973 and 1974 the FCO was still offering jobs as District Officers in the South Pacific and in Hong Kong. In the South Pacific independence for the Gilbert and Ellice Islands, the Solomon Islands and for the Anglo-French condominium of the New Hebrides was on the horizon; so for those territories applicants were offered only three-year renewable contracts. For Hong Kong the applicants were still being offered career appointments.

The two members of the Selection Board in addition to myself as Chairman were retired colonial officers, one of whom as a young man in the Colonial Service had himself been a highly regarded District Officer in the Solomon Islands. Tom Russell later became governor of the Cayman Islands. We decided to look particularly for young people with first or second class degrees from 'red-brick' universities. The process was an education for me. I came away from the experience convinced that no young person should be allowed to go to University without having first had a gap year. What the candidates did during a gap year made them that much more mature and credible as young persons who had some idea of what the jobs we were offering might involve.

There was some licence in what candidates were asked during the interview: 'How do you think you might manage going on foot through the jungles of the Solomon Islands to administer justice to the natives?' or 'What do you think of the prospect of going around the Gilbert and Ellice Islands by canoe for a week or two?' Some of the candidates seemed to have at least some idea of where these territories were; so they were asked what they had read about the South Pacific islands. The invariable answer was *A Pattern of Islands* by Arthur Grimble. It became clear that Grimble's book with his somewhat romanticised tales of his own experiences as a junior member of the Colonial Administrative Service in the Gilbert and Ellice Islands was the only relevant book to be found in university libraries at the time. My grey-haired old colonial officer colleagues' view of Grimble was 'That man did a lot of harm.' Much later I decided that Noel Coward's *Uncle Harry's Not a Missionary Now* might have been closer to the real thing. I have in recent years paid two one-day visits to Kiritimati – also known as Christmas Island. It is interesting as an example of a truly remote Pacific island. The visits also made me realise how one day on the island might be just long enough. It was an example of needing to bear in mind that no matter how idyllic such an island might be with its beaches, blue sea, sunshine and coconut palms, for most people used to modern society it is always important to know that one has the facility available to escape from a paradise. Grimble's book is a good read – but not a useful guide for young people thinking of making a living in the Pacific islands.

An unfortunate example of a young person who had wasted a great deal of family and public money, as well as several years of a young life spent studying the wrong subject, was the excellent candidate who came to us with a Bristol University first class honours degree in mathematics. The Board members asked her, 'But what about a mathematics career?' – to which her answer was that she was not at all interested in mathematics. 'So why did you study mathematics at university?' The answer she gave was that she had been good at mathematics at school and her teachers thought that that was what she should study at university. Whether the teachers' motivation was a genuine belief in what was best for the individual student, or whether it was a case of what might prove to be to the greater glory of the school she had attended, we couldn't tell. While this young woman was the extreme case, several of the other candidates similarly proved to have no real interest in the subjects in which they had graduated.

The best candidates for the adventurous jobs in the South Pacific were those who had made good use of a gap year. One was a girl who had spent her time travelling across India by bus; another the boy who spend a year teaching rugby in the south of France. Those two were examples of candidates selected because of their obvious maturity. At one point my colleagues reminisced along the lines of 'Do you remember when we used to get ex-National Service candidates? So much more mature.' For the unusual jobs for which we were recruiting, such candidates were much better prospects than the young 'straight from university' candidates, no matter how good their university degrees might be. I came to realise just how fortunate I had personally been in having four 'gap' years, so that by the time I embarked on study for a university degree I knew exactly what I wanted to study and why. Teachers are almost certainly invariably thinking of what is best for the student. But are they the right people to advise on careers for particular individuals? Of what careers do most teachers have first-hand experience other than teaching? The gap year should be mandatory. What a young person does with that year will shape their future. The year could teach them about a lot of work they would realise they would certainly not want to do for a life-time career, while possibly opening up their ideas for a field of employment at which they will not only be successful but which will make their whole life more worthwhile.

The Selection Board for the last few jobs of Empire was unanimous in deciding to recommend for appointment the candidate with the first class honours degree in mathematics. The difficulty was that she was a female. No female had ever been accepted as a trainee District Officer by any British colonial administration in the Pacific. My colleagues and I thought however that it was worth a try recommending her to the New Hebrides where there was a chance that the French might already have appointed a woman to their half of the administration of the condominium. I hope she made it. She was a pleasure to interview; but also a sad lesson in how many young people have wasted time and money studying subjects that they were not really interested in and that would prove of little help towards developing a life-time career that they would find fulfilling.

After some time in Gibraltar & General Department I really couldn't find enough to do, so I persuaded Personnel Department to move me. The move was to Assistant Head of Information Administration Department. One of the main functions of IAD was to deal with the FCO's 'information' budget. This meant negotiations with HM Treasury at a time when substantial cuts were being demanded in the context of the annual reviews of the Public Sector Borrowing Requirement. 1974–75 was a time of budget deficits, galloping inflation and high unemployment.

IAD needed to negotiate such matters as the Foreign Office subsidy to the BBC World Service and a financial contribution to Reuters news gathering activities. So my commercial and economic background and my accountancy came in quite useful. Indeed it taught me that the supposedly brilliant people in HM Treasury sometimes make mistakes with their basic mathematics. I greatly pleased my Head of Department and the Deputy Under Secretary by negotiating an extra £400,000 out of the Treasury when I could show that Treasury had been incorrect in their elementary arithmetic. Another lesson learned is that highly intelligent and well-educated officials, who may have first class honours degrees but who lack experience of the world outside government service, are often not good at figures and often do not understand how the outside world will seek to interpret government rules and regulations. I thought back to the lesson in Indonesia as to how fifty very clever people were making up the foreign exchange regulations to help the struggling economy while five thousand equally clever people in the business community were working out how to make money out of the same rules and regulations.

My involvement with central government budgeting was during the period of great public borrowing and spending reviews/cuts of the 70s. Forty years later the economic and government financial situation of most Western governments, including both in the UK and Australia, would seem to be a case of *déjà vu*. The subsidy to the BBC World Service was a perennial problem. How did the Foreign Office justify making a subsidy to the BBC World Service in the first place? It was I suppose a left-over from the propaganda efforts of the 1939–45 War. The annual Public Sector Budget Review process did not begin objectively by planning from a zero budget and working out what was needed. The process started from how much each heading of expenditure had received the year before. It then became a case of trying to work out how much could be cut to meet the government's 'across the board' percentage policy; or how much HM Treasury could be persuaded to accept as the minimum on which a department could manage in the coming year.

In the case of the BBC World Service there was no rational departmental analysis of what the World Service was doing and what it was worth. No one wanted to say how much of the expenditure by the World Service went on little more than providing cricket scores to the expatriate British living in Malaysia or other foreign parts. It was simply a case of arguing over the total amount of money. The BBC World Service might be allowed a 2.5 per cent increase for inflation because everyone else was getting 2.5 per cent. But beyond that general increase expenditure cuts had to be made. In the case of the World Service the task for IAD in the FCO was to persuade the BBC to accept any cuts at all.

One of my *Yes Minister* stories derives from my time with IAD. Lord Goronwy Roberts, a Labour Government Minister of State at the FCO, had occasion to receive a trade union delegation. The delegation wanted to express the union's concern at possible reductions in staffing at the BBC due to cuts in the FCO funding. As Assistant Head of the relevant Department I was asked to attend the meeting and to make a note of the proceedings. The Minister had with him his Private Secretary, Roger Westbrook, plus myself as departmental note-taker. The trade union was represented by a three-man delegation. When the meeting was over I returned to my office to write up an account of how the meeting had progressed. I made a note of what the delegation had said and, more importantly, what the record would show the Minister had said. When I had completed three or four pages of notes and had them typed, I sent a copy to the Minister's office for his approval. The original of my note came back to me with Lord Goronwy Roberts's handwriting in the margin saying, 'I had no idea I said it so well.' The series *Yes Minister* has I am sure been viewed on more than one occasion by every civil servant in the land. Like all good fictional comedy and all good theatrical tragedy, *Yes Minister* is just a slight exaggeration of real life, an exaggeration that nonetheless enables its audience to identify with what they are seeing.

The BBC was in the 1970s and undoubtedly still is, very good indeed at rounding up its lobby to argue publicly that whatever cuts were to be made in expenditure on the nation's foreign affairs there should be no loss of jobs at the BBC. It was tough to take on the BBC in those days. The BBC had loud and active supporters in Parliament and elsewhere. As soon as any suggestion of cuts surfaced the whole BBC lobbying mechanism got to work very quickly.

Unlike my experience of working in the bureaucracy in Canberra, where I enjoyed the work but not the city as it then was as a place in which to live, I thoroughly enjoyed my spells of working in Whitehall. There were of course differences. Charming as Canberra was as a city, it was no London. Also perhaps my view was affected by the fact that I knew I would not be permanently in an office in Whitehall. My stays in the Foreign

Office were interludes between postings to the outside world. It was certainly stimulating to feel that one was working at the centre of a great international city where the issues were often of significance in world terms. Also there was the experience of working with people from the generations that produced some of the finest British diplomats. But our time in London also provided some useful lessons in the attitudes of our children towards boarding school and towards the repeated movement of their parents from one part of the world to another.

My view became that anyone who does not believe in boarding school education should not pursue a diplomatic career. Our American colleagues tended to keep their children with them at post, relying on a local American or International school to provide a suitable education. But when an American diplomat moved from one post to another it meant that their children changed home, school, and friends and started all over again to fit in to new surroundings, with new teachers and new social groups. While the argument might be that it was better for a family to keep together, there was also the problem, for more senior officers at least, that diplomatic life with its heavy social commitments could mean that the parents were not always aware of what their children might be getting up to when not actually in school.

With two children born in Tasmania and two in South Africa, and with the expectation of moving from one country to another every few years, Margaret and I had agreed early on in our wandering life that boarding school was the answer. Fortunately for us the British Diplomatic Service supported that system with very good education allowances.

A matter of concern for us was that the two younger children had never had experience of living in a house that we owned. There had always been the constraints on childhood activity that go with living in a rented home or in official accommodation. So we decided that we should go as far as our budget would allow and buy a home of our own to occupy while our stay in London lasted. In a home that we owned it would not matter so much if one of the children drew on a wall, spilt something on a carpet or wanted to modify a room or furniture to allow for the setting up of toys, or indeed wanted to kick a ball around the garden. So we stretched our finances to the limit and bought a modern town house in Tristan Square, Blackheath. It was just large enough to accommodate all four children during school holidays. It had a garage that proved just the place to set up tables to accommodate a model train layout. We felt that here was the chance for Peter and Sarah to settle down in a real home of their own and where we could also accommodate Pru and Roger during the holidays.

I have a very clear memory of being in the garage helping to set up the model train layout just a few months after moving in when Peter turned to me and said, 'Where are you going next, Dad?' This convinced me that boarding school was not a problem and in reality provided much more stability than if we kept the children with us and moved them from school, friends and house every few years. They were quite settled to have the same teachers, the same group of school friends, and the same general living environment year after year. Spending the school holiday with us two or three times a year was enough so long as the house contained some of their books and other belongings and there were some familiar pictures and household bits and pieces about. The stays with us, whether Brazil or Cambodia, or later South Korea, meant that they also had interesting stories to tell when they returned to school for the next term. There is also the possible situation that the tensions such as those that develop between parents and teenage children in particular are worked out at school rather than at home. We are at least speaking to all four of our children and they to each other!

After just eight years in the Service and at the end of three years as Assistant Head of Department I cannot have done too badly. I was told that my confidential report referred to me as a 'good negotiator'. In 1976 I was promoted to Grade 4 (Counsellor grade) for my next posting. That was I came to realise rather good considering I had spent just eight years in Grade 5 compared to the much more usual twelve years or so in the same Grade for someone recruited to the Administrative Grades straight from Oxford or Cambridge. It was a first step towards catching up with those who had entered the Diplomatic Service much earlier in life than I had. The next posting was to be as Commercial Counsellor which once again involved filling the role of 'Deputy Head of Mission'. The job had all the appearance of being a most interesting appointment: and so it proved to be.

CHAPTER 8

Through the looking glass. Seoul: 1976–80

M Y THREE AND A HALF YEARS AS Commercial Counsellor at Seoul in South Korea, from 1976 to 1980, provided me with what was undoubtedly the most rewarding professional experience that I ever had from the point of view of commercial and economic work. Once again I was also in post as Deputy Head of Mission, with regular spells as Chargé d'Affaires for three months each year when the Ambassador took his annual leave. Those additional duties added some memorable experiences outside the sphere of my main day to day official responsibilities.

I had learned from previous experiences that before one starts on practical matters of commercial work, or indeed of any aspect of diplomacy, it is important to understand the culture in which one is expected to work. To add to the lessons I had learned in Singapore, Jakarta and Phnom Penh, Korea provided me with many new lessons in how Asian cultures need to be understood not only by Western politicians but also by those seeking to do business on a worthwhile basis.

One of the early thought-provoking incidents in Seoul was at the Australia Day reception at the Australian Ambassador's residence. I found myself in conversation with a tall distinguished American who was introduced to me as the President of the highly respected and long-established Jesuit Sogang University. In appearance and bearing he reminded me of the missionary base manager who had rescued me from the Biak airport in Indonesia in 1967. I am quite certain my new acquaintance was exactly what he said he was; unlike my Biak host whom I couldn't help suspecting was CIA – after all, as the R and R centre for missionaries from throughout Indonesian New Guinea, my rescuer on that occasion was in the ideal position to know more than anybody, including the Indonesians, about what was going on throughout the huge area of what was then called Irian Barat.

Not being sure what subject I might diplomatically and usefully raise with a distinguished Jesuit I asked, 'How much impression is Christianity making on Asian thought processes?' To my great surprise the immediate answer was: 'None at all.' The distinguished Jesuit went on to explain that in a harshly ruled oriental society such as China, or in a society such as sternly ruled South Korea was at the time, joining a foreign church was a relatively safe form of dissent. Being a member of a foreign church, particularly the Roman Catholic Church, meant that a dissident was not alone; he could count on some support and comfort from a worldwide organisation that might be expected to speak up for him and his fellow oppressed 'Christians'.

My new acquaintance went on to say, 'Somehow Christianity has to adapt to the Asian mind.' I could but wonder that after the hundreds of years the Jesuits had been working in Asia such a conclusion seemed an extraordinary admission as to how little progress they had made in the cause of Christianity. In subsequent years I often reflected on that final remark about adapting Christianity to the Asian mind. Then, about ten years after I left Seoul, I returned to Korea on a business visit. I chanced to pick up the current edition of the local English language newspaper. There on the front page was a headline: 'Ancestor worship to be permitted.' The news item reported that the Catholic Church had agreed that 'Ancestor worship is permissible providing it is preceded and is followed by a Christian prayer.' Some adaptation to the Asian culture had clearly been recognised as a worthwhile move.

While my previous experiences in South East Asia were helpful in understanding Korean society and the business community, those earlier experiences by no means gave me the whole story when dealing with a society which I maintain was at the time the most Confucian society on earth: a highly disciplined society at every level. Confucianism has been corrupted to some extent in China by conflicts of the past hundred years, including Mao's efforts to change Chinese society by drastic policies such as the Cultural Revolution and through the later unintended consequences of the 'One Child' policy. But in South Korea in the 1970s the country was for the great majority of the population still a society where only disciplined families who observed the traditional rules of Confucian obligations and responsibilities could be sure of surviving. Surviving a harsh winter was a battle in itself when for long periods temperatures in Seoul went below $-20°C$ before taking the wind-chill factor into account. Each family had to be self-sufficient in its food supply through winter and in ensuring there was sufficient fuel on hand to keep the traditional under-floor heating going throughout the long cold season.

The traditional under-floor heating, identical in principle to the heating system installed by the Romans in colder climates such as along Hadrian's Wall in northern England, itself required disciplined behaviour on the part of a home's occupants. The discipline included never entering the house with anything on the feet other than socks or soft slippers. Visitors to Korea often thought the practice of being required to take their shoes off before entering a Korean house was a quaint custom. In reality the practice was to ensure that no harsh surfaces on shoes scratched the waxed paper with which floors were covered. One scratch through the floor covering of paper could result in carbon monoxide gas entering from the under-floor heating channels and silently killing a whole family in their sleep. The US military radio AFKN repeatedly broadcast warnings to US servicemen 'living on the economy' (i.e. living with Korean girl friends) to ensure that their living space was well ventilated. Carelessness in observing the local customs could kill.

An important aspect of Korean society in the 1970s was still the annual rice harvest. It was a rule that workers in the city should be given a week's leave to go to the country to help harvest their family's rice crop. Harvesting the rice was then followed by the production of the family's winter supply of *kimchi*. Together with just an occasional piece of fish or chicken the store of *kimchi* had for centuries past been a key to food supply for family survival through the harsh winters.

At the relevant time of year the pavements of side streets in Seoul would be stacked high with piles of cabbage, piles of red chillies and piles of dried prawns. These ingredients, with the addition of a substantial component of garlic, would be made into *kimchi*. The pickled product was then packed in large earthenware jars of the 'Ali Baba' size and style. The full jars would be buried in the family's back yard at just the right depth to ensure that they would be kept cool but mostly importantly would not freeze. Frozen *kimchi* would lose the vitamins and other food value that made it such an essential component of the winter diet. Trouble started when South Korea began to build multi-storey apartment blocks for the large number of people coming to work in the cities. I began to notice the traditional large jars of *kimchi* being kept on the small balconies of such high-rise blocks. Storing the jars in the open air meant that when the temperature dropped well below freezing the *kimchi* would freeze and lose its key food value. The problem was dealt with by learning how to preserve *kimchi* in cans and sealed glass jars.

Kimchi is not to every Westerner's taste, either to eat or to smell. I developed a real liking for the taste of the chilli and the garlic. Just writing about it and my mouth begins to water! But *kimchi* presents some problems at home. I recently found a Korean store in Hobart stocking the product. When I bought a small container of it I had to wrap it in several layers of plastic and then keep it in the refrigerator with the wine rather than in the one holding food. From time to time I take a taste but have to do so in the fresh air on the porch outside the kitchen door, and then hope that a good mouth rinse will minimise the effect on my breath.

New diplomatic arrivals in Seoul found the smell of *kimchi* difficult to take. I remember the New Zealand ambassador's wife, Marjorie Cunningham, a good friend of ours to this day, standing with us waiting on an upper floor for the elevator after lunch at the Seoul Club. When the lift door opened it was well occupied by several pretty young Korean office workers. One move towards the door of the open lift and our companion stepped back in horror. 'I'm not going in that lift!' The strong smell of garlic was only too obvious: a new and unpleasant experience for a New Zealander recently arrived in Seoul.

Westerners notice that pretty Korean girls often laugh or giggle while holding a hand over their mouth. The gesture is not one indicating shyness. The hand is there to cover up the 'dragon's breath' that goes with having eaten *kimchi*.

Only a disciplined and tough society could have survived Korea's history of invasions and Japanese occupation. The threat from North Korea was ever present and dominated security concerns in the 1970s. It was soon after my arrival in Seoul that, entirely by chance, it was discovered that the North Koreans had been building large tunnels under the demilitarised zone with the intention of being able, in the event of open conflict, to release large numbers of their soldiers well behind the first South Korean defence lines.

The 'no-fly' zone over the presidential palace and city centre meant just what it said. One evening as I was about to leave the office there was, without any warning, the noise of a huge anti-aircraft barrage fired into the air over the busy city from guns that I had not realised were installed on the roofs of many buildings in the vicinity of the Embassy. The barrage was fired because an American aircraft of Flying Tiger Line had either carelessly or foolishly entered the 'no-fly' zone. No time was wasted giving a warning to the pilot. 'The price of peace is eternal vigilance' was then, as it remains to this day, an absolute for South Korea.

Confucian principles went right through society. This affected relationships within Korean companies; it affected relationships between Korean companies and their government; and it affected their attitude in dealing with Westerners such as those of us in the British Embassy as well as our business and other visitors.

The key traditional Confucian relationships and their associated obligations, all of which naturally refer only to men, which were the absolute keys to Korean social relationships when I was in Seoul are:

Ruler to Ruled: The Ruler has an obligation to provide security for his people so that they can get on with their own affairs in safety. The Ruled have an obligation to be loyal to the Ruler and to obey his orders. The observance of this rule was evident in general local acceptance of the stern rule of President Park Chun He.

Father to Son: The father has an obligation to provide his son with a secure childhood and the best education possible to prepare him for life. The son has an obligation to do what his father says he should do. An example of this was in the early years of the Daewoo Group. When I arrived in Seoul the Daewoo group of companies was managed by two brothers, both of whom I got to know well. One of the brothers was a regular guest at our house. The older brother had been lecturing in economics at a first class university in the USA. He told me that his father had sent a message telling him that he must return to Seoul to help his younger brother run the expanding family business. So the older brother gave up what he was doing successfully and happily on his own in order to return to Seoul to become a key figure in the early very successful years of the Daewoo Group. It was many years later before he returned to university life in America.

Older Brother to younger Brother: An older brother has a responsibility to help his younger brothers in life: Younger brothers have an obligation to accept direction from their older brother. The classic instance of this in the 1970s and 80s was the Hyundai Group. The Chairman of Hyundai Group was Chung Yu Jung and each of the companies in the group was headed by one of the four younger brothers or, as there were not enough brothers, one company in the group was headed by a son-in-law and another by a brother-in-law. Chung Yu Jung's rule of the Hyundai group of companies was as strict, if not more so, than the presidential rule of the country by Park Chun He. Whenever Chung Yu Jung departed on an overseas visit every brother and other Hyundai company president went out to the airport to see him off – and to be ready to receive any last minute instructions. The arrangement worked according to plan until Chung Yu Jung died. Tensions then developed, apparently because not all of the younger brothers were from the same mother.

Teacher to Student: The teacher must devote himself to teaching and mentoring his students to the best of his ability. The student has an obligation to study hard, to respect the directions of the teacher and also to have some responsibility for the care of his teacher in later years. A specific example of the student's responsibility for his teacher came to my notice from my Indonesian-Chinese friend Carlo Tabalujan, who in his autobiography describes how during the Japanese occupation of Indonesia he and a classmate took a grave risk by leaving occupied Jakarta and going into the rural area of west Java to help one of their teachers evade the Japanese authorities searching for him.

Classmate to Classmate: Classmates have an obligation to be loyal and to help each other. One example of this was again the Daewoo Group at the time I was in Seoul. There were nearly thirty different companies but, as a visitor pointed out, there were only two Kim brothers. I explained that careful examination of the structure of the Daewoo Group of the time would show that every subsidiary company was headed by a classmate of one or other of the two brothers.

Confucian relationships can be vital to survival in difficult times. If a Chinese or Korean is alone and has not even a classmate to help him, he will have no one to whom he can turn to for help. An individual will feel little if any obligation to help or feel responsibility for 'outsiders', though there are sometimes exceptions when a person, even a foreigner, has had a long-established relationship as a particularly good friend of a family.

The key relationships were as important in business as in family and general society. The people in the relationships were not only the people to whom an individual owed obligations but also the people an individual could trust. One of the problems with many Asian businesses is that when they get so large that they cannot be controlled by the founding family, the business has to employ outsiders in management positions. Outsiders have obligations of their own, obligations that may well transcend loyalty to their employer. We had an example of that in the Commercial Department of the Embassy where it was discovered that a locally engaged member of staff was giving under the counter help to a Korean businessman who was one of his classmates from university.

The opposite to respect for the relationships was the 'shock horror' when the obligations were ignored or one party was unfaithful to the other. The extreme example was the assassination of President Park Chun He. I remember the Ambassador expressing grave concern that the assassination would cause ructions in Korean society generally. My view was that the assassination itself would not be a problem for Koreans to accept. It was a case of how else did you change the head of such a government when it began to become apparent that 'Little Father' had passed his 'best by' date and had no obvious successor. What really shook Korean society at the time was that Park Chun He was assassinated by one of his own classmates from military school – a classmate he trusted so much he had made him the head of his own CIA.

It was in itself an aspect of oriental culture that on the one overseas visit made by Park Chun He as President he should take with him not just one or two ministers and one or two advisers, but virtually his whole cabinet and the government's key economics team as well. It was considered important to show his hosts that by taking a large entourage he was demonstrating how important he considered the Burmese to be. Burma was especially important in that it was the only country that I remember inviting President Park to pay a visit in the days when Park was seen by much of the world as a little more than a hard-line dictator.

There was a tragic consequence of President Park's desire to develop a close relationship with the Burmese government of the time by showing how important he regarded his visit to that country. There was to be a ceremony at which the visitors were seated on a covered platform to see a parade of some sort. The whole of the Korean party, with the exception of President Park himself, were in their places on the platform when a bomb planted by North Korea exploded. While missing their key target Park Chun He, the bomb killed several of his Ministers and a number of the Korean government's highly regarded advisers. One of those killed was Kim Je Ik, the key Korean economic planner with whom I had a good relationship. He was one of the significant number of highly intelligent Korean graduates from Stanford University and from Harvard who were responsible for engineering the remarkable economic and industrial development of South Korea. I used to pay regular visits to him at the Ministry of Economic Planning, visits that I tended to regard rather as one might attend tutorials at university.

When I visited Kim Je Ik he would explain current Korean policy and intentions with regard to the economy. On one occasion he explained that Korea had been taking a close look at the economic history of Canada and of Argentina, two countries that in the 1930s had seemed to be among the most prosperous. With respect to Argentina my friend said, 'We have come to the conclusion that the Argentinians thought they had "arrived" and didn't need to go on working so hard. We don't want our people to stop working hard just yet, so we will keep a tight control of the economy and continue to keep a grip on consumer spending for a few more years to come.'

Park Chun He was anathema to any liberal-thinking foreigners of the time, but in my recollection no one ever accused him or his government of corruption. The phrase 'poor but honest' could be one description, a description that certainly applied also to Vietnam when I went there a few years later. One reason for the absence of serious corruption at the time might well have been that Park himself had virtually no family and no personal hangers-on seeking to profit improperly through their relationship with the country's President. Park had a young son who was a nonentity in the Korean army. He also had an outstanding daughter, but no wider family to take advantage of his position for the purpose of facilitating graft.

To Korean society Park Chun He was the stern 'Little Father', a strong leader whose name was associated with harshness in enforcing presidential edicts and the imposition of punishments on those who did anything that was considered to be against the security of the country. But to balance the stern father figure Koreans could look for a more sympathetic figure in the President's wife: the 'Yin and Yang' that maintain balance in oriental life.

The death of Park's wife when she became the unintended victim in an assassination attempt on him was a particular tragedy for Korean society. Without the balance between stern 'father' and his 'softer' wife there was something missing from Korean society. This was considered so important that their daughter assumed the role of her mother. She did so to the extent of having her hair styled the same way and dressing in exactly the same style as her late mother. The daughter became the symbol of balance between the hard leader and a softer half. The daughter gave up whatever career she might have had in mind in order to play the role of her murdered mother as the comforting personality in the collective Korean society. She had graduated in chemistry in the United States and was recognised as being both clever and beautiful. She became highly respected, later gaining her own following when democracy developed in South Korea and a political group saw her as an asset when campaigning for votes.

I gradually came to realise that whatever the West might think, Park Chun He was not so much a dictator as a stern Chairman. The President made very few decisions himself but acted on the advice of government Ministers. The key was that once the President had put his 'chop' on a decision that decision became absolute law that was not to be questioned.

Not long after President Park Chun He was assassinated Margaret and I were having a quiet evening at home watching *M*A*S*H* on black-and-white AFKN (American Forces Korean Network) when there was a noise outside. When Margaret exclaimed 'What was that?' I, being rather tired after a strenuous day as Chargé d'Affaires while also managing an active Commercial Department, was absorbed in the activities of the characters on the screen. I replied quickly, 'Just someone dropping a load of planks on a nearby building site.' A few minutes later the telephone rang. It was the Defence Attaché, to tell me, 'There has been some shooting in your area.' Apparently one group of generals were disputing with another group of generals the succession to their late colleague Park Chun He. One group of classmates from military college were disputing with another group of classmates.

There was not much any of us could do that night to find out more about the conflict. It would have been foolish to have set off during curfew, even with diplomatic car number plates, to drive around the city out of curiosity, or even to get to the Embassy Chancery to send a telex message, at a time when the capital might be about to explode in conflict between factions of the military.

But I did recall my experiences in Cambodia. Firstly, that in the event of internal conflict one of the first things likely to happen was that telephone contact with the outside world would be cut off. Secondly, that journalists might have found an instant means of communicating some news to their offices in London. Thirdly, that the news media would then call the Foreign Office to ask for what reports the FO had received from the Embassy about the safety of British subjects in Seoul. Fourthly, that colleagues in the FO would be (a) embarrassed, and (b) annoyed, if it had to be admitted that there had been no word from the Embassy about such dramatic developments. So I immediately picked up the telephone and called the Resident Clerk, doing so while hopefully pre-empting the cutting off of ordinary communications with the outside world. All I could say to London was: 'There has been shooting in Seoul in a suburb where key generals are known to live. No British citizens or members of the Embassy staff are thought to be in danger.' That was quite enough to enable the Resident Clerk or the Information Department to show that the Embassy was fully aware of what was happening and had kept London instantly informed. Having done my duty I went back to watching the activities of the characters in *M*A*S*H*.

There were other aspects of Korean society that needed to be understood if setting out to do business with South Korea. One important matter to be borne in mind is Korean antipathy towards Japan and almost anything Japanese. The difficult relationship between Korea and Japan is of very long standing, related especially to Japanese occupation of the Korean peninsula from 1904 to 1945. The Japanese tried hard to destroy the Korean culture and language and were very brutal in their attempts to do so. An example that helps understand the Korean attitude towards things Japanese came when an elderly business contact and I were being driven across the main Seoul city square. My companion pointed to the pavement and said, 'My father had his head cut off just there by a Japanese officer because my father refused to speak Japanese to him.'

The Korean antipathy towards anything Japanese was well illustrated at a different level when Margaret and I invited to dinner the local agent for British General Electric. BGE were providing the conventional generation equipment for two of the first Korean nuclear power stations. As a wedding present we had been given a Japanese print – possibly by Hiroshige. The print followed us around the world and in Seoul we found a place for it where it fitted just inside the front door of our residence and thought no more about it. When the President of Whashin Tiger Industries arrived for dinner, accompanied by his two English-speaking sons, I opened the front door to them to be almost immediately confronted by a clearly upset guest speaking rapidly in Korean. The elder of the two sons, clearly embarrassed by his father's angry words, said, 'My father wants to know why you have that Japanese picture in such a prominent place inside your front door?' After a further exchange between father and son the son told me, 'My father will send you a Korean picture to hang instead of that Japanese one.' He then got out a tape measure and noted the measurements of the piece of wall where the Japanese print was hanging. The dinner then proceeded amiably. Margaret and I now have a Japanese print and a Korean picture facing each other across the dividing arch of our sitting-dining room, so that if conversation lags over dinner we are able to explain their story to our guests.

Asian businessmen can be extremely loyal customers when you have done them a favour and mutual trust develops. One might also say of Korea that to help a British company get into the Korean market at that time, one could advise the company representatives that they should rehearse all the usual arguments for buying British machinery or equipment and then, when the potential customer had analysed all the details of the product on offer, the British salesman could add the phrase, ' . . . and we would like to help you beat the Japanese.' With Koreans that phrase could almost certainly guarantee a successful business deal!

On the other hand there was the occasional problem when I recommended a good Korean company as a potential agent for a particular British company. The British company would reply: 'We cannot appoint that Korean company as agents as Korea is part of the sales territory of our Japanese agent.' Such a British exporter clearly knew nothing of the history of Korean-Japanese relations. There was no way a Korean would willingly import a British product through a Japanese agent if an alternative was available from any other supplier.

There were many successes for British business during my time in Seoul and they provide a series of stories that illustrate what a 'commercial' diplomat can do to help if he understands both the local culture and the way business works. I do not want to impose on present readers my full reserve of 'business' stories, but one particularly gratifying trade success was to sell large quantities of British steel under the noses of the highly efficient Japanese steel industry. How that happened is perhaps worth re-telling in this memoir.

During one of my times as Chargé d'Affaires a Korean (Pom-Su Yi), whom I had not met or heard of before, came in to see me and said he would like to represent British Steel. First of all I thought that his idea was a lost cause if ever there was one. But then he said, 'No, I don't want to represent everything that British Steel produces, just one or two items where I think I know what I am doing, and where I think I can get business.' He explained to me that Daewoo Group had recently taken over the huge Okpo shipyard project on the southern coast of South Korea. I was familiar with the huge shipyard because I had been the only outsider invited to the handover ceremony when Daewoo, at the urging of the Korean government, had taken over the huge project from Korea Shipbuilding Company of Pusan. I shall certainly not forget sitting among a large group of Korean executives and VIPs on the covered dais while torrential rain drenched a brass band valiantly playing appropriately inspiring tunes as the ceremony proceeded.

Daewoo were continuing the construction of the Okpo shipyard. In the shadow of the 1974 oil crisis and the seven-year closure of the Suez Canal, the yard had been designed to build million-ton oil tankers, tankers that would take oil round the Cape of Good Hope. No million-ton vessels were actually built at Okpo or anywhere else but several 500,000-ton ships were built.

Associated with the shipyard's construction huge amounts of steel were being imported. The project was being financed primarily with Asian Development Bank money. Daewoo had therefore been required to call tenders, under ADB rules, for a large quantity of H-beams – steel beams in the shape of the letter H. The beams were to be used for holding up the roofs of the huge warehouses associated with the shipyard. My Korean contact said that he knew that on a previous tender the only people who bid were three or four Japanese companies. The Japanese steel companies were now so confident that they would be the only people who would bid again, that they would jointly up the price of their steel for the H-beams on the basis that, having worked it out between them which company was going to get the business, they would have no competition (a cartel in other words). Knowing what was going on, Mr Pom-Su Yi wanted to put in a bid for British Steel.

I managed to persuade the managers at British Steel in Humberside to give Mr Yi a price. On the day the successful tender was announced Mr Yi came in to see me and said, 'I was able to walk into the room and tell the Japanese I had got the business, before they even opened the tenders. My only mistake was that I did not put the price up high enough. The Japanese had loaded their price.' Losing the business was a terrible loss of face for the Japanese steel industry and its local representatives, especially as they had been beaten under their very noses by, of all people, the notoriously inefficient and expensive British nationalised steel industry.

1. At the beginning of diplomatic adventures. Margaret, Roger and Pru about to leave for South Africa 1962.
By courtesy of The Mercury, Hobart

2. Brasilia, 1969–72: waiting, with friend, to receive guests. Hugo was quite harmless unless
he stood on his hind legs to lean on you.

3. June 1962: representing Australia at the last Queen's Birthday Parade ever held on the lawns of Government House, Nairobi was a nostalgic experience of the last days of Empire. We are to the right of the row behind Kenyatta, Mboya and other Kenyans soon to take over the government of an independent Kenya.

4. 10 August 1962: Singaporeans had Independence thrust upon them. A complete surprise to all.

5. We took 'Commonwealth' responsibility for entertaining Singapore's first and long serving Foreign Minister, Mr S. Rajaratnam, when he visited Brasilia; a visit that coincided with a rare visit from Rio by the Defence Attaché Brigadier Winstanley.

6. Cambodia 1972–73: Angkor Wat was occupied by the Khmer Rouge with Siem Reap airport within mortar range. Widening a dirt road to provide a landing strip had uncovered this small temple previously buried by an immense bamboo thicket.

7. Accompanied by the Defence Attaché Colonel Michael Dracopoli and a Cambodian military escort, I was taken to see the newly discovered temple. We each received an AK47 as a souvenir.

8. Seoul 1976–80: Margaret could play up to stars of stage and screen. Rolf Harris was in Korea to make an early tourism promotion film in 1977. Margaret and our children played the part of visiting tourists.

9. Margot Fonteyn danced on her 59th birthday when the Royal Ballet visited South Korea. Margot and her mother, Hilda Hookham, came to lunch with other members of the ballet.

10. Dining in Houston with Margot Fonteyn and her husband at the home of Joy Rothwell, a cousin of Margot. Hugo Arias would have been President of Panama but an assassination attempt paralysed him from the neck down. Margot spoke for him, but his eyes twinkled whenever there was humour in the conversation.

11. The Consul-General's residence in Houston was the most pleasant of all the diplomatic accommodation we occupied. Good enough for entertaining Royalty, astronauts and film stars but not embarrassingly ostentatious.

12. The three of our children who were with us in Houston were quickly put at ease by Princess Anne when they were introduced to her. From l to r: the twins Peter and Sarah, and Roger, 1982. By courtesy of Houston Chronicle

13. The only time I have featured in a newspaper cartoon – recognizable by the balding head perhaps as both escort and bag-carrier it would seem – on Princess Anne's arrival at Denver 1982. By courtesy of Mike Keefe, Denver Post

14. *Discussing Australian politics with Shirley MacLaine at the party Lynn Wyatt gave for Sam Wanamaker who was touring the USA in support of his Globe Theatre project.* By courtesy of Houston Chronicle

15. *Princess Margaret's first visit to my 'territory' was to open an exhibition of Her Majesty's Leonardo da Vinci drawings. I made a great effort not to be in front of HRH, while at the same time trying to ensure that the group was proceeding in the right direction.* By courtesy of Houston Chronicle

16. *Lady Bird Johnson and Margaret at a three-day symposium held in Austin to mark the 50th anniversary of FDR's first election as President. I was there to read a message from HM The Queen Mother.*

17. *George Thomas, Speaker of the House of Commons, came to stay for the nine days of the 1981 'British Festival' in Houston*

18. *'The way we were.' Our Texas years were certainly enjoyable. Not just Texas of course but also New Mexico, Colorado, Oklahoma, Louisiana and Arkansas.* By courtesy of Houston Chronicle

19. 1985–87: From a delightful 'southern' residence in Houston to an equally delightful but unusual residence in Hanoi

20. The dining room where US Senate and Congressional delegations were given breakfast, and the Soviet Ambassador and his wife came for dinner

21. In the life we have led, getting all six of the family together has been a problem for many years, Roger in Hong Kong, Pru in Hobart, Peter in London and Sarah in Queenstown, New Zealand. Sydney 1988.

My Korean friend told me that Daewoo executives were delighted. The transaction had saved them US$300,000 – and they would like to do more business with British Steel. However, Daewoo said they could not, unfortunately, order more H-beams because they didn't really need any more H-beams; but they did need T-beams. However, if they wanted to order T-beams they would have to go through another Asian Development Bank tender process. As the Japanese would never risk losing face twice, the Japanese steel companies would 'give away' their steel the next time round, just to make sure no other manufacturer beat them to the business and caused yet further embarrassment. However, Daewoo Group had told Mr Pom-Su Yi: 'We want to do more business with British Steel rather than the Japanese – so what we can do is to order more H-beams at the same price as the previous tender, without going through a new tender process. We can then cut the H-beams in half to make T-beams.'

It was an extremely difficult exercise explaining to British Steel in Humberside that Daewoo's attitude was: 'British Steel have done us a marvellous favour by saving us a lot of money. We are loyal customers. We would like to do more business with British Steel. So we would like to order more H beams at the same price as before and then we will cut the beams in half to make T-beams'.

I heard a couple of years later, when I met one of the British Steel people involved, that what eventually happened was that British Steel sold Daewoo more H-Beams and then themselves cut the H-beams in half for the Koreans. The business continued for some years and Mr Pom-Su Yi and his Nan-Gi Trading Co Ltd prospered as the agent for British Steel. Later British Steel also did excellent business in steel piling for underground railway construction in Seoul, not just for one underground line but for several.

There was a great deal of goodwill towards Britain as well as to Australia and New Zealand in both government and business circles. The contribution by Britain in the Korean War was often referred to while the small memorial to the valiant defence by the Gloucestershire regiment at the Battle of the Imjin River was carefully maintained by a local high school.

In business it was well known that Britain was supplying the conventional generating equipment for the first two nuclear power stations built in South Korea and had provided some major equipment for the first Korean steel mill. Even more significant was the British contribution to the Hyundai shipyard and to the Hyundai Motors project

The Hyundai shipyard was designed by the British firm Appledore. An Appledore representative told me it was a designer's dream to be able to design a yard on a green-field site, something they would never have been allowed to put into practice in the UK because of trade union opposition and planning obstacles. Appledore did it for the Koreans, backed up with centuries of British experience of shipbuilding. Appledore produced what has become one of the most successful of all modern shipyards, one that is generally accepted as now the largest shipyard in the world and by 2009 the largest builder by far of the ultimate in high-technology cargo ships, the carriers of liquid natural gas. But in the early years Hyundai's skills were essentially in the basic business of building ship hulls using what was then the cheapest steel in the world, made by the Korean steel mill POSCO.

Britain also designed and, in the person of George Turnbull − a legend in the British motor industry − helped commission the first Hyundai motor-car factory. The Hyundai Motor Company was seen by the British Department of Trade & Industry as a threat to the British motor industry; especially perhaps because it was, like the Hyundai shipyard, being built on a green-field site, in this case having the advantages of the many years experience that Britain had in motor vehicle manufacturing. The British Department of Trade & Industry saw any help being given to the Korean car industry as an almost immediate threat to British vehicle manufacture. London had visions of cheap Korean cars on British roads within a year or two.

I did my best to explain to DTI and anyone I was in touch with in the British motor industry, that it would be some years before any Hyundai cars would appear in Europe. For one reason Korean technology in assembly needed years of testing: an aspect highlighted when we went for a visit to the Hyundai plant and my wife was invited to drive one of the very first Hyundai 'Pony' cars as it came off the assembly line. The gear lever came away in her hand as she tried to change gear while the car was moving steadily along the wharf outside the factory, dangerously close to a drop into the water.

It is not only in relationships between businessmen that understanding different cultural values is important. There also needs to be an appreciation of what might be the real objectives of a government, rather than the wording of some particular official regulation or decree. A favourite cartoon of mine appeared in the Korean English-language press while I was in Seoul. It was one of an American series involving two characters, 'Frank and Ernest'. The first frame of the cartoon showed one of the characters coming down from the mountain dressed as Moses, bearing two stone tablets under his arm. The caption to the first frame read, 'These are the law.' The second frame of the cartoon showed the same character pointing to a huge pile of stone tablets in the corner. The caption to the second frame read, '. . . and those are the government guidelines.' I felt that the cartoon must have been drawn especially for Korea as it was at that time.

In some societies the law as stated by formal government edict or published regulation, is not as important as the often unwritten guidelines. It is necessary to look beyond the published statement to determine what may be the real objectives of the government, rather than to read the letter of the announced policy as people in Britain might interpret it when translated into English.

I admired much of what I learned of Korean culture because it explained how Korea has survived and continues to survive. Understanding the culture in which I was working also helped greatly when advising British businessmen how to do business with South Korea.

CHAPTER 9

A lighter side

T HERE WAS VIRTUALLY NO PUBLIC entertainment in Seoul at the time
Margaret and I were there, certainly none likely to attract the
foreigner's general interest and none that a visiting businessman might wish
to spend an evening watching or alternatively might want to describe in
detail to his colleagues and family when he got home. There were cultural
shows and events at the Western–style Walker Hill complex but they were
aimed mainly at the US military on an R and R break.

The cultural shows did have some interest for me in that I soon realised
that the folk dances in Korea were almost the same as the folk dances in
Indonesia, in Malaysia and in Cambodia. Then I recognised that all such
dances in that part of the world reflected the system of agriculture – the
'wet rice' culture – so it was not surprising that in each country the dances
followed the pattern of the farmers' lives. The dance cycle would begin
with a dance depicting the sowing of rice; then a dance marking the
replanting of the young rice; then there might be a quieter dance reflecting
the period when the villagers waited for the rice to grow; then a harvesting
dance; then a dance depicting the winnowing of the harvested rice; and
finally a celebratory dance to mark the completion of the cycle, usually
taking the form of a happy wedding ceremony. Not surprising that there
should be a similarity of village dances throughout that part of the world
where lives revolved around the progression of rice from seed planting to
harvesting.

Korea did have a form of entertainment that I had never seen anywhere
else, though at times I did describe it as a Japanese geisha party in a
somewhat less formal style; much more of a 'night out with the boys' event:
the Kae Sang party. My first experience of a Kae Sang party was definitely
a cultural shock. The host, Chung Se Yung, was a younger brother of
Chung Yu Jung, Chairman of the Hyundai Group. Chung Se Yung was
President of the Hyundai Motor Company, a Hyundai group company that
had a close current business relationship with Britain. The party was held
at a very upmarket entertaining pavilion in the hills on the outskirts of
Seoul.

On entering the dining hall guests were seated at a large long table, with its top very close to the floor. The Korean hosts sat on one side and the foreign guests on the other. Even then, when I was much younger than I am now, I was having trouble sitting down just a few inches off the floor. I was thankful for the chair frame provided especially for foreigners. The design of the frame allowed me to stretch my legs out under the table and lean back for some of the time. Each of the guests had their personal Kae Sang hostess who sat on their right-hand side dressed in beautiful traditional Korean garments. The hostesses' main task was to keep the guest's drink glass filled. But the hostess was also there to keep her guest amused and entertained, a responsibility that I discovered included giving my leg a discreet squeeze from to time.

It was a fun evening with a certain amount of ribaldry, a lot of drinking, and some guests occasionally being given a hug by their personal Kae Sang hostess. When the eating had finished there was music and it was made clear the custom was to stand and move with one's hostess to one end of the dining hall for twenty minutes or so of Western style ballroom dancing. It was considered very bad manners for a guest to indicate that he might like to dance with any of the pretty girls other than the one designated as his hostess. I was beginning to wonder where it was all going to end when, as if a whistle had been blown, we all stood up from our places, not the easiest of task for some of the Westerners present, said a courteous goodbye to our respective Kae Sang companions and then all went home. Thank goodness for the 10 p.m. curfew! Even if as a diplomat I was excused the curfew I was pleased that all the Koreans hosts had to be off the street and at home by 10 o'clock. I did sometimes wonder whether all the Koreans actually went home or had somewhere else to fill in the curfew hours until 4 o'clock in the morning.

I soon got the knack of attending both small and large Kae Sang parties without coming to any serious harm, though some of the smaller parties could certainly be a strain on one's liver. I have little doubt some visiting businessmen may well have got into serious trouble. I soon found that almost without exception my hostess for the evening would seriously keep my best interests in mind once I made it clear I liked my whisky watered down. The usual practice was to drink many toasts during the evening but to drink them out of a small liqueur glass, while a larger glass of whisky and water served as a 'reservoir' from which one's hostess would refill the small glass ready for the next toast. All would go well so long as the toasts were all drunk with watered down whisky; but Chung Se Yung and one or two others had a bad habit of every now and again proposing a toast to be drunk in 'crude oil', which meant drinking neat whisky.

Another problem visitors had to watch out for was the practice of each one of a group of several Korean hosts proposing a personal toast for the visitor to join in, with both parties downing the contents of one of the small glasses filled with whisky. It was most important that the foreign visitor insisted that if one host proposed the toast all of the other Korean hosts had to drink to it too. Otherwise the visitor could find himself drinking several toasts while his hosts each drank one only.

Generally the Kae Sang party was a form of entertainment popular with all Korean men from all levels of society – and probably quite popular with the hostesses for the fact that they were well paid. Most were good fun and one or two provided opportunities for business matters to be discussed. But perhaps most important, as in other societies, was the attitude towards foreigners from a different culture. Does the stranger enjoy the things we enjoy? If he doesn't enjoy the 'fun' we do, can we expect to develop a good working business relationship with the newcomer? It all helped in developing good personal relationships – and I do not mean with the Kae Sang hostesses. Attending a series of Kae Sang parties brought home to me the adage that 'a diplomat gives his liver for his country'.

The traditional entertainment could be expensive for a Korean host. Even a small Kae Sang party with three or four Kae Sang hostesses, imported liquor and an elaborate meal, could be costly for a small to medium sized businessman. I advised visiting businessmen from time to time that they should not be surprised if their Korean agent asked for a higher rate of commission than that which the businessman's company paid their representatives in other parts of the world. The agent might have some expensive entertaining to do. The larger more formal versions of the same kind of hospitality, whether given by Hyundai or by the government, could be very expensive indeed.

There were other aspects of Korean culture that affected day-to-day life. We learned early on in our stay in Seoul that no Korean man would in normal circumstances take instructions from a woman. This became a practical problem at the office when we recruited three outstanding young Korean women to work in the Commercial Department. Korean business-men found it very difficult to take them seriously or to take instructions from them if we sent a group off to Singapore as official guests to a British trade exhibition there. Whatever Miss Chung might tell her charges about where they should be and at what time they should meet to catch the bus to the exhibition, some of the men in the group would simply ignore her. For me Mrs Min, Miss Chung and Miss Chang were stalwarts of the office. All three stayed on for many years after I left and Mrs Min was awarded an honorary MBE after twenty-five years service.

The Korean culture that placed men above women, or at least allowed the men to think they were superior to women, spread into our domestic arrangements. No tradesman would take any notice of what Margaret said she wanted done about the house, nor would notice be taken of what our first Korean housekeeper told him needed doing because she was not 'of a certain age'. But then one day I opened the front door in answer to a knock and found outside a middle-aged Korean woman we did not know but who simply said, 'I have brought Mrs Kim to be your housekeeper.' Mrs Kim was our guardian angel for the next three years. She was a white-haired grandmotherly figure who always wore Korean traditional clothing when going out from the house and who, when in the house, dressed in a starched white apron just as one might have expected to be worn by a character in the TV series *Upstairs, Downstairs*. The key was though that Mrs Kim not only looked like a grandmother but that she was over sixty years of age. Every Korean tradesman who ever came to the house would be most respectful to her and always do whatever task she asked him to do. While I had my work to keep me enthusiastic about being in Korea, it was Mrs Kim who made our home life comfortable and agreeable throughout our stay there, especially for Margaret. Mrs Kim's water chestnut soup became a regular feature at our dinner parties.

The American community in Seoul, with their huge military presence, tended to look very much after themselves, though we were given honorary membership of the American Embassy Club which had premises inside the central city Itaewon military base. The Club provided an agreeable alternative location for the occasional Western dinner for just the two of us or with an American colleague. The Americans took food hygiene very seriously: even the lettuces were flown in. Otherwise the main social event at the time for the expatriate community was the St Andrew's Day Ball. Because of the curfew the Ball, held at the Seoul Club city premises, was timed to start at 9.30 p.m. and did not, could not, finish until 4 a.m. The manager of the Chartered Bank, Jim Medley, was an excellent 'caller' for the Scottish dancing.

For Margaret and for me the most memorable non-commercial events were those that happened around the visits of the Royal Ballet and the Royal Opera. The Ambassador, Bill Bates, was not one for cutting his leave short just because the Royal Ballet or the Royal Opera might be visiting the post, which meant that Margaret and I had some great experiences and got to know some remarkable people.

In 1978 Margot Fonteyn accompanied the Royal Ballet on a visit to South Korea. She danced in Seoul on her fifty-ninth birthday. To the Korean method of counting that was however her sixtieth birthday. A sixtieth birthday marks a new status in the life of any Korean, but especially in the life of a Korean woman. Margot danced to a piece especially choreographed for her, rather than join in the corps de ballet traditional items, but her style and beauty were as spellbinding as ever. When she ended her dance the announcement of her sixtieth birthday was broadcast in Korean into the huge theatre. There was a great gasp from the audience and a swarm of young Korean women rushed to the edge of the stage to try to touch her. I remember seeing a puzzled expression on Margot's face. Not understanding the Korean language announcement she did not appreciate the significance to Koreans that she should be able to dance on what was such a very significant milestone day in the life of any Korean woman.

Margot Fonteyn's visit gave us the opportunity to entertain to lunch both her and her mother Hilda Hookham: a delightful personality with whom Margaret got on extremely well. We were given Hilda's London address with a view to making contact when we were next there but sadly she died not that long after her visit to Seoul. The names on the page in our guest book for 17 May 1978 include not only Margot and her mother but also those of Monica Mason, Susan Lockwood, Gerth Larson and others from the company. Michael Soames also came to Seoul. He no longer danced in the real sense of the word, but having watched him in the role of the major-domo in *Swan Lake*, I have ever since said, 'I would like just to be able to walk like that.' I gather from later experience of *Swan Lake* in St Petersburg that the role may have been written into the Royal Ballet production especially for Michael Soames. The first ballet I ever attended was at Covent Garden some twenty-five years before the Royal Ballet came to Seoul. The programme on that much earlier experience made a great impression; it included Cézar Franck's *Symphonic Variations* in which the dancers were Margot Fonteyn, Moira Shearer, Beryl Grey, Michael Soames and two other male dancers whose names I regret I have not been able to remember.

We attended a number of functions given in Seoul for the ballet company, but members of the company had a poor time socially because of the curfew. We had an introduction to one of the coryphées, Julie Lincoln, of whom I am reminded every time I see the 'Dance of the Cygnets'. It was when we attempted to set up some form of post-performance party for the non-principals in the company that the young dancers quickly pointed out that their normal social life only began at 11 p.m., by which time not only was the curfew in force in Seoul but the services in the hotel in which they were staying had closed down completely by 9.30 p.m.

It was having the opportunity to stand in the wings during rehearsals and during a performance that led me to realise that while the dancers may all be smiling for the audience as they dance into the wings, the moment they are off stage they appear to be about to collapse, covered in perspiration and looking as though they have just finished playing an hour of strenuous squash. The term 'sweating swearing swans' described them well.

Just by being 'head of post' when important events took place meant that we had quite a number of opportunities to become friendly with many special people, of whom Margot Fonteyn was one of the first. Margot signed her photograph to us as Margot Fonteyn; our visitors' book she signed as 'Margot Fonteyn Arias'; and when she wrote a letter and two personal notes to us she signed them 'Margot Arias'. A sequel to getting to know her in Seoul occurred a few years later in Houston when Margot passed through and we were guests with her at two private 'family' dinner parties for just six people. At the later of those two dinners her husband Hugo Arias was with her. The assassination attempt against him when he was a potential President of Panama had left him paralysed from the neck down. He was still a handsome man. He could not speak but could make a throaty sound. His manservant wheeled him to the table next to Margot's seat and she fed him and acted as his voice. Margot's devotion to her husband was clearly by then the major concern of her life. It was an extraordinary experience, because while he could say nothing both Margaret and I were sure that his eyes twinkled when there was humour in the conversation. We both went home that evening certain we had been guests not only with Margot but with a charming, handsome and most agreeable dinner companion, her husband.

Our guest book page for 9 September 1979 records another group of guests that we had to our home in Seoul. The page is headed by the signature 'Olivier', followed down the page by Colin Davis, Geraint Evans, Jon Vickers, and John Tooley. The following pages include the signatures of Forbes Robinson, Patricia Payne and ten or twelve more members of the Royal Opera, all of whom came to an informal dinner we gave for members of the Royal Opera when that company visited Seoul. Missing from the guest book are the signatures of Monserrat Caballe and a 'young Spanish singer', José Carreras. They both came with the Royal Opera to sing *Tosca* on the first evening of the programme in Seoul, but both went on to Japan as soon as their performance was over; so we did not have the opportunity to entertain them. They may not be in our guest book but I recently found a faded copy of the programme for *Tosca*, printed half in English and half in Korean and bearing both of the signatures that did not make it into our book. I relate elsewhere how Laurence Olivier's signature came to be in our guest book on the same occasion as the stars of the Royal Opera.

The Royal Opera visit to Seoul provided additional interesting insights into Korean society in the days of President Park Chun He. Before the opera company arrived I gave a small dinner party for the local sponsor, Kim San Man, proprietor of a major local newspaper, the *Dong A Ilbo*. Paul Findlay and another member of the opera management team in Seoul as an advance party for the opera company were also present. Included in the guest list of ten was a distinguished Korean woman prominent in matters concerning Western opera. She spoke quite strongly at the dinner table to suggest that the Royal Opera should not have included Benjamin Britten's *Peter Grimes* in the programme. She insisted that that opera 'would not be understood; the programme should have been kept to operas well known to Koreans'. When the visit took place there was no doubt whatever that it was *Peter Grimes* and the music of Benjamin Britten that was the outstanding success of the week, particularly with young Koreans. This Asian affinity with the music of Benjamin Britten is, I was told, of significance in Japan where there had been a society devoted to his music for some years.

I was again Chargé d'Affaires when the Royal Opera arrived in Seoul. In the days leading up to the opening performance I received a telephone message from the Blue House asking me to call upon the President Park Chun He's Private Secretary. When I had made my way through the tight security I found that the Private Secretary wanted to discuss a possible visit by the President to a performance of the visiting Royal Opera company. It was explained that the President had never before attended a perform- ance by a visiting foreign company such as the Royal Opera and that if he did attend he might come for just part of a performance. I took the opportunity to suggest Act One of *Tosca* as perhaps offering most drama, rather than *The Magic Flute* or *Peter Grimes*. Not until some time later did I realise that the political background to *Tosca*, with the involvement of the secret police and torture, especially in Act 2, was perhaps a little too topical for President Park's regime at the time.

I was then asked to describe the procedure followed when HM The Queen attended a performance by the Royal Opera. I explained the pattern of the audience arriving and taking their places in the auditorium before Her Majesty arrived; then standing for the national anthem when The Queen entered; then sitting down again before the performance could begin. The Private Secretary then said that for security reasons they would not be able to say just when the President would arrive. I immediately had visions of President Park arriving just when Monserrat Caballe was in full voice. The thought of the whole performance being required to shut down for some minutes in the middle of an act filled me with some alarm. So I explained very diplomatically that there would be no problem if the President arrived at one of the intervals in between the acts.

The next day I was asked to call again at the Blue House. This time I was told that if the President attended it would be wished that in addition to the Korean national anthem the orchestra would play the 'President's Hymn': a cultural innovation obviously acquired from the Americans. I said that that could be done, but the orchestra would need to see the score in advance. The problem then was that I was told that there was only one copy of the score and that was a classified document: if they released the score to me and to the orchestra there might be a security leak to the effect that the President could be going to the opera at some time during the week. A dissident might in turn, intentionally or otherwise, leak it to North Korean agents. It was agreed that what would be done would that be that on the day of the final rehearsal the score of the 'Hymn' would be sent to me secretly and I could then discreetly show it to Sir Colin Davis while the orchestra was rehearsing. It was assumed that at the rehearsal only the musicians and a few others would recognise the additional music being tried out.

The confidential music arrived at the Embassy in a 'Secret' package. I set off immediately to the Cultural Center taking the package with me. I showed it to Colin Davis, who was at the podium conducting the final rehearsal. I explained the sensitivity of the matter. Colin Davis took a quick look at the music and immediately said, 'No problem.' He passed the sheets of the score around the orchestra and within a minute or two the orchestra were playing the secret music loud and clear. From the darkened body of the theatre, that I had assumed would be completely empty, came a burst of applause. There were in the theatre some two thousand students who had been invited to listen to the orchestra rehearsing. So much for trying to keep secret the President's interest in attending a performance of the Royal Opera. In democratic countries one could almost count on some of any group of students to boo or jeer upon hearing music carrying a similar association with their nation's political leader; so I found intriguing that at a time when Westerners, especially those of a liberal inclination, were excoriating the government of Park Chun He for its dictatorial harshness towards any form of dissent, the reaction of a large body of Korean students unexpectedly hearing their President's personal hymn was to applaud.

In the event President Park attended both the first and second Acts of *Tosca*. His daughter came with him and from where I was sitting immediately behind the presidential box I could see her explaining the 'action' to her father. I learned later that that opera performance was the first Western cultural event Park Chun He had ever attended. It was almost certainly his last. He was assassinated not long afterwards.

VIP visitors to South Korea were gradually increasing in number, but not all came while I was 'in charge'. Two VIP visits with which I had some involvement included a Kae Sang party in the visitor's local programme. One such visit provided a lesson in what could go wrong. It would never have happened if I had been in charge!

Someone persuaded Sir Edmund Dell, then Secretary of State for Trade and Industry, that South Korea was becoming important enough to justify a visit by him in his official capacity. The Koreans were delighted at this, their first such high level visit by a British Minister. They set out to be as hospitable as they knew how. That meant including in the programme a Kae Sang party on a grand scale for about thirty guests paired with thirty

Kae Sang hostesses of the highest reputation. Ambassador Bill Bates had assumed control of the visitor's arrangements as he rather hoped no doubt that familiarity with members of a high level mission might improve his prospects for employment after retirement. I was as Counsellor Commercial included in the guest list for the major social event of the programme – the Kae Sang party.

I found myself seated on a low cushion on the opposite side of the table to Sir Edmund Dell, his host, and the Ambassador. I was placed some little way to the side rather than immediately opposite the VIPs. This meant that I could watch Sir Edmund closely yet was far enough away to be out of range of his immediate attention. Sir Edmund, as the guest of honour, had clearly been paired with a most senior and highly regarded Kae Sang hostess. He was not sitting next to some giggly youngster but with someone who undoubtedly saw herself and was seen by the Korean host to be the local equivalent of a most respected geisha of Japan. Nonetheless, as I watched from my side of the table I had not the slightest doubt that Sir Edmund's leg had received a gentle squeeze somewhere above the knee. Sir Edmund's face began to assume a rather disconcerted expression, then a positively grim one, while the poor lady trying to be attentive, but who spoke no English, was showing growing concern at the response her traditional attentions were producing. The Korean Minister and the Ambassador, and I for that matter, went ahead enjoying dinner in the manner to which we were accustomed on such occasions.

When the meal was finished it was the usual practice at such parties for all guests, accompanied by their respective Kae Sang hostesses, to go to one end of the large room to participate in what can most easily be described as 'clutch and shuffle' dancing at close quarters. I watched the Ambassador and our host stand and proceed in the same direction as all the other guests. I cautiously stayed in my seat to see what the Secretary of State would do. His expression suggested that he did not think much of the way the evening was progressing. Sir Edmund, followed by a clearly now desperate partner, went to the opposite end of the room and sat on a long formal couch facing the length of the room at the other end of which the happy crowd were dancing to big band music. When seated next to him the distinguished Kae Sang hostess, no doubt seeing her reputation and her career about to crash, appeared to be making matters worse by trying to sooth him down. At that point I stood up with my hostess and moved quietly to the back of the dancing crowd where I would not be noticed.

The next thing I saw was the Ambassador and one or two visiting British Department of Trade officials gathered together in what looked rather like a rugby scrum. I thought I had better move close to give an appearance of availability to support my Ambassador if called upon. The drama was that 'The Secretary of State wants to leave!' How to explain to the host Minister that his guest wanted to break up what was probably the most expensive party the Koreans had ever given for a British visitor? This was a party the Korean officials and others were happily enjoying at the Korean government's expense. The decision was hastily made to attribute the problem to the guest of honour being so very tired after his long flights and the excellent but intensive programme he had followed during his visit. So we all went home.

The Ambassador later told me that when he accompanied our VIP visitor to the airport the next morning Sir Edmund did not say a word to him throughout the drive. I was convinced the problem was that no one had explained to the Secretary of State the unusual but quite harmless customs that went with a formal Kae Sang party.

A little later on in our stay in Korea, soon after the visit by Sir Edmund Dell that led to embarrassment for both guest and host, there was an occasion where the mention of a Kae Sang party sounded alarm bells for me. I was, yet again, Chargé d'Affaires. I received a message from the Foreign Minister's office saying that the Foreign Minister would like to discuss with me the programme for the forthcoming visit by 'Prime Minister' Edward Heath. (Another little practice Koreans acquired from the Americans is that of continuing to give public figures, including Ambassadors, the courtesy of their past title.) I immediately sent a return message saying I would be available to call at the Foreign Ministry at any time, whenever it was convenient to the Minister. No; that would not be necessary: the Foreign Minister thought it would be a good idea to discuss the programme over dinner one evening. So an evening was agreed and I went off to dinner feeling rather pleased; it was quite a privilege for me as a mere Chargé d'Affaires a.i. to be the sole foreign guest at a small dinner party with the Foreign Minister. It turned out to be a very exclusive Kae Sang occasion. The Foreign Minister, plus two of his senior officials, me, and four charming Kae Sang hostesses. It proved to be a quite sedate but very pleasant dinner party – no 'clutch and shuffle' dancing. I don't recall there being any squeezing of knees either. The Foreign Minister at the time was a most distinguished Korean in both appearance and manner: a truly worthy oriental gentleman. He had been Ambassador to the Court of St James's for a while. We had interesting and worthwhile dinner conversations.

When the meal itself was finished the Minister said, 'Well, we should discuss the programme for the "Prime Minister".' His next words were: 'There should obviously be a Kae Sang party.' My instant reaction was to open my mouth preparing to say something along the lines of 'I'm not sure that would be quite in Mr Heath's style,' when the Foreign Minister said, 'After all if a man doesn't like a Kae Sang party he is not a man, is he?' So I shut my mouth and said nothing to contradict my host. I gather that when the time came Mr Heath dealt with the Kae Sang experience quite well; no doubt because the Ambassador had learned a lesson from the earlier visit by Sir Edmund Dell and had carefully briefed the 'Prime Minister' on how the occasion would proceed.

I have the impression that democracy and slightly more open government, let alone some female emancipation in South Korea, has meant the demise of the traditional Kae Sang entertainment as I remember it. A pity if that is so; but with an increasing number of women in diplomacy and in commerce the pattern of the all male Kae Sang party might lose its character. It was becoming something of a problem even in the 1970s because an increasing number of diplomatic wives were demanding explanations of just what went on during such evenings. The questioning became sufficiently pressing for the Hyundai company to arrange a Kae Sang evening for husbands and wives. The event led to a great deal of confusion for the Kae Sang hostesses and my recollection is that it wasn't much fun.

As far as Margaret and I were concerned I regret having to say that Edward Heath was not the most charming of visitors. In one post or another we had visits by Ministers of one political persuasion or the other, Lords Mayor of London, as well as numerous 'captains of industry'. Over the years when I was HM Consul General at Houston we were also closely involved when I had responsibilities for or was associated with a total of nine visits by six different members of the Royal Family. With one exception all the visitors we dealt with throughout my career were most pleasant towards Margaret and me and most appreciative of what was arranged for them. That exception was Edward Heath.

'Prime Minister' Heath wasn't rude or outwardly unpleasant. He was just indifferent, not just to us but also to his hosts the Korean government. The

Koreans provided a military aircraft to fly him, accompanied by me, for a long day to the south of the country to show the 'Prime Minister' two of the industrial projects of which they were most proud – each of which had some direct connection with Britain either by way of design or in the supply of equipment. The visitor showed no interest; he asked not a single question, not even as we toured the British-designed Hyundai shipyard at Ulsan.

From the Hyundai shipyard we travelled on by road to Pohang a little further north along Korea's east coast. When we arrived at the huge POSCO steel mill, the President of POSCO received us in the company's large display room where, behind the curtained windows, an audio-visual presentation took place in conjunction with an excellent model display of the whole complex steel mill. Miniature illuminations progressed from one side of the model of the site, where the iron ore and coking coal were unloaded, through the modelled coke ovens and furnaces on to the final stage where the mill produced sheet steel. When the display of the miniature steel mill was complete the curtains were drawn back and through the wide semi-circle of windows we could see the whole of the actual steel mill itself replicating the model. It was very well done. But there was then silence. Heath said not a word and looked uninterested. After a minute or so of silence one of the officials asked, 'Do you have any questions, Prime Minister?' The response was something of a grunt followed by: 'How much money are you losing on this steel mill?' The Koreans laughed and said, 'We are not losing money, we are making profits.' I suppose some might say Heath's attitude to the steel mill could be excused by his experiences of dealing with nationalised British Steel and its trade unions. But as a visitor for whom his hosts had gone out of their way to provide an interesting visit, Margaret and I thought that his whole manner as a guest was boorish and an embarrassment to us as representatives of Britain.

At the end of my posting to Seoul I went from Korea to 'something completely different'. In September 1980 I was appointed to Houston as Her Majesty's Consul General for Texas and five other states in the south-west USA.

CHAPTER 10

Recognising the talent but not the man

D URING OUR YEARS IN SEOUL the regular spells as Chargé d'Affaires a.i. provided Margaret and me with a wide range of experiences that were, at least from the story-telling point of view, certainly rather more entertaining than my responsibilities for trade promotion. Most of the experiences were pleasant ones, or at least were not connected with tragedy in any way. An exception to the more cheerful experiences came about as a consequence of the murder in Ireland of The Earl Mountbatten in 1978; but that too had associated with it a story worth telling.

When news of the murder came to the notice of the small British community in Seoul a member of the community asked if a memorial service might be held. It was a proposal to which I readily agreed. I took on the responsibility for organising a service to be held in the crypt of the small Anglican cathedral, which is sited immediately outside the gates of the British Embassy compound in the centre of Seoul. Korean language services were held in the main body of the cathedral while the crypt was set aside for English language services.

In arranging the Order of Service it seemed appropriate that I, as nominal head of the British community in my role as British Chargé d'Affaires a.i., should deliver the eulogy. It would then I considered be appropriate that the First Lesson should be read by the Defence Attaché, while to demonstrate my progressive and politically correct non-sexist credentials I asked Thora Medley, wife of the manager of the Chartered Bank, to read the Second Lesson. Thora was chairman of an informal British women's group that had been organised to provide a means of organising modest social events for the few British wives living in Seoul at that time.

Having allocated responsibility for the formalities of the Service I then prepared a notice to be sent to all the Commonwealth citizens known to be in Seoul. There were Canadians, Australians and New Zealanders and one or two others, with a total of about two hundred at the time. I also sent copies of the notice to the recently opened Hyatt Hotel, having heard that Laurence Olivier had just joined a film production company staying there.

The presence in Seoul of the famous actor Lord Olivier was not widely known. His 'employers' were anxious about the health and security of their star. I was aware of the film production because some weeks earlier I had been invited to a large dinner reception given by the Japanese backers of a movie to be based on General Macarthur's role in the Korean War. The dinner was itself remarkable only for the fact that I sat next to the Japanese host who spoke not a word of English, while Raquel Welch sat at the far end of the very large table. The beautiful movie actress was so far away from me that I cannot claim to have exchanged so much as a word with her. She would definitely have been a more interesting dinner companion than my host. My recollection is that Raquel Welch at her end of the table looked as bored as I was at my end.

Shortly after the circulars about the Memorial Service went out from the Embassy the Ambassador's secretary passed a telephone call through to me in the Ambassador's office telling me that there was an Englishman wanting to speak with me. I may explain that when I acted in the Ambassador's place I used his office and his secretary. I also had his entertainment allowance which I discovered Margaret and I made rather better use of than he had been doing. On this occasion, when I picked up the telephone I heard a rather frail voice say, 'It's Larry Olivier here.' He thanked me for the notice of the Memorial Service and went on to say, 'Dickie Mountbatten was a good friend of mine and I should very much like to play some part in the Service.'

My immediate response was to suggest that my caller take over responsibility for giving the Address. The reply came: ' No, no. I would lie awake all night worrying about what to say.' 'What about reading one of the lessons?' I asked. 'Yes, that I should like to do.'

I undertook to send Lord Olivier a clearly printed copy of the 'script' taken from Isaiah 25: 6–9. Having settled that particular piece of casting I next rang the Defence Attaché to tell him that he had been up-staged by Laurence Olivier. I did not however tell anyone else. I wanted to be sure that members of the community came to the Service because it was a memorial for Admiral of the Fleet The Earl Mountbatten, not because they expected to see the great actor in the congregation.

On the day of the Service my wife and I arrived at the cathedral flying the flag on the official Daimler, the large and impressive model, ideal for formal occasions. Koreans were sure that the car was a Rolls-Royce – a mistake about which neither I nor anyone else in the Embassy did anything to disillusion them. On taking our place in a front pew I could see Laurence Olivier and a couple of 'minders' already seated across the aisle. His hair had been darkened for the part he was playing as General MacArthur. I would not have recognised him if I had not been expecting to see him there.

The Service went well. Instead of Laurence Olivier staying up most of the night composing the Address, that task had fallen to me. I was rather pleased with my effort and kept the original of the text, including last minute amendments, among my souvenirs. But the only comment I received afterwards was from a businessman in the congregation who asked, 'Did London write that for you?'

As we were standing in the cathedral courtyard introducing our distinguished lesson-reader to a few very surprised members of the congregation, a member of the community came up to me and asked, 'Where did you get that marvellous preacher to read the lesson?' No one in the congregation had recognised the person of Laurence Olivier, but they had had no difficulty in recognising the talent.

'Larry', as he asked us to call him, stayed in Seoul on at least two occasions. The film he was acting in turned out to be being financed by the Moonie organisation through an associated Japanese company. Whether Larry knew the source of the million dollars he was said to be paid I do not know. The film was eventually given provisional release in New York under the title *Oh Inchon*. It was so badly panned by critics that it has to my knowledge never been seen or heard of again. Margaret and I are sorry about the fate of the film only because our younger son Peter and a friend, both in Seoul for the summer school holidays, had obtained well-paid employment as extras, filling the role of GIs wading ashore under enemy fire. Sadly, both for tragedy and for the financial earnings of Peter and his friend, a young Korean extra stepped in the path of a tank. It was then realised that the film company should not have been employing anyone under the age of sixteen.

Larry was in Seoul on one of his filming visits when the Covent Garden Royal Opera Company was present. He told us that he knew several of the visiting company personally; but when we offered to take him to their performances he said that his health was not good and his contract required that he did not to go out at night. His health did indeed appear to be quite fragile. He said however that while he could not attend evening performances he would very much like to go to the opera rehearsals. So for a week I sent the office Daimler to pick up Margaret who in turn collected Larry to take him to the Cultural Center and then to sit in with him at the rehearsals.

The rule imposed on the film company's very expensive asset, insisting that he did not go out and about at night, was broken on one evening. When we gave an evening informal dinner for the opera principals and a few others, Larry came to join us. It was convenient that our residence was 'just round the corner from the Hyatt Hotel'. Instead of putting our fragile guest in the main room among the other thirty or forty guests we sat him in my study and brought a few of his friends in from time to time to sit and talk with him. That is how our personal guest book came to have a page headed by 'Olivier' and followed by a long list of prominent opera personalities.

Larry invited Margaret to have lunch with him on one of the days she took him to the opera rehearsals. She has never forgiven me for intruding. We sat for a fascinating three and a half hours over lunch, his choice for the meal being *fettucini alfredo*. He may have been rather frail and in delicate health, but there was certainly nothing wrong with his appetite. Larry told us that while in Korea he spoke every day with Joan Plowright, his second wife, and he mentioned that his son Tarquin was working in Hong Kong.

It was a privilege and a delight to spend time with such a man who by the end of a couple of weeks we could claim as a friend. It was a special delight for Margaret who had seen Laurence Olivier and Vivian Leigh perform at the Theatre Royal in Hobart while she was at school. Sadly the great actor died before we had any opportunity to see him when we returned to London for a few weeks before moving on to our next overseas post.

CHAPTER 11

Houston: 1980–85

A S FAR AS LONDON'S PROTOCOL WAS concerned my appointment was as 'Her Majesty's Consul General'. Usage was however to refer to me as 'British Consul General'. The appointment was as Consul General for the six States of Texas, New Mexico, Colorado, Oklahoma, Arkansas and Louisiana: an area as large as Western Europe. There was a lot of travelling to be done.

After leaving Seoul in early summer Margaret and I in due course arrived in Texas in September 1980 to take up residence in what we have always regarded as the best official accommodation we have ever occupied. Some far-sighted colleague had bought a house in the top suburb of Houston and arranged for it to become the official residence for successive British Consuls General. The house was just right. It provided a good family home in the most expensive suburb without being in any way ostentatious. It was large enough to entertain fourteen to a seated dinner and sixty or more for a 'stand-up' reception. The house was sited on what was often described as the only hill in River Oaks. The building had been designed in the distinctive 'southern' style usually associated with Louisiana. Number 930 Kirby Drive might stand on its own as a symbol of the British presence, dignified but not stately, and by no means an embarrassing display of ostentation at the expense of the British taxpayer.

In years prior to our arrival Houston had for a long time been designated a 'hardship' post for British diplomats, as indeed was Washington DC. The principal consideration for such designation as 'hardship' was based on the average temperatures and humidity in the hot season. It wasn't until the 1970s that the Foreign Office discovered air-conditioning, by which time the British characterisation of Houston as 'hardship' was part of the local folklore and would from time to time be mentioned to me by service-station attendants and other ordinary Houstonians. It would indeed have been a hardship post before the introduction of air-conditioning. But when someone would ask me how we managed in the Houston climate I would answer 'What climate? It is ten yards from my air-conditioned house to my air-conditioned car; and ten yards from my air-conditioned car to my air-conditioned office building.'

If ever a motor-car could be considered essential it is in Houston. When I first met Margaret her father was driving a fine 1938 Buick and I had long determined that the mark of having 'arrived' in the sense of proving that I could maintain her in the style to which she had been accustomed would be when I could buy our own Buick. So some thirty years after our first meeting I had no doubts about choice of car in Texas. I went directly to the nearest Buick dealer to buy a 'Le Sabre'. It was one of the anomalies of conditions of employment that as a Grade 4 Consul General there was no official car. With a few exceptions all official and private driving was in my own vehicle. The trouble was that in Houston one family car was certainly not enough, so I almost immediately had to go back to the dealer and buy a small Buick for Margaret's own use. Later, when three of our four children came to live with us, it quickly became clear that with two adults and three 'near adults' in the house, life was impossible with only four motor cars. So we ended up with five motor vehicles, one or two of which were definitely not a credit to the River Oaks neighbourhood.

The obvious commercial interest in Houston for Britain was, and I am sure remains thirty years later, the oil and gas industry. But it wasn't a commercially active posting in the direct trade promotion sense. In Houston we were not helping British exporters in the detailed and specific way that the Commercial Department did at the Embassy in Korea. We were working more to create a favourable general environment in which British business could operate and do business with the worldwide oil and gas industry. The trade promotion of exports was undertaken primarily through the subsidiary Consulate in Dallas, situated close to the Dallas Trade Center. My activity as Consul General on the other hand had a strong element of public relations to it, not just in Houston but throughout the area for which I had responsibility. That side of my work became particularly important during the period of the hunger-strikes by IRA prisoners in Northern Ireland and throughout the Falklands War.

I arrived in Houston at the beginning of the oil boom and bust period from 1980 to 1985. When I arrived in Houston executives of the major oil companies showed me how their future plans were based on the assumption that the price of oil would go to $40 a barrel. By the time I left in 1985 the same executives were talking about $14 a barrel. At the same time the 'rig count', the number of oil drilling rigs operating within the USA, itself a key measure of activity in the oil industry, had dropped dramatically. But in 1980 there were many opportunities opening up for British industry, not least in the great oil shale projects on the western slopes of the Rocky Mountains in Colorado where billions of dollars were being spent on three separate projects, all on the assumption of $40 a barrel oil. A few years later all such projects were closed down. New townships with names such as 'Parachute' and 'Rifle', that had also been under development, complete with high schools for the anticipated expanding population in a quite remote area of the western Rockies, were under the process of being converted into retirement villages. Thirty years later the oil boom and bust sequence occurred all over again.

It was surprising that in spite of the large number of British firms with offices in Houston by 1980 there was when I arrived no local British 'business association'. At my first lunch with several from the British business community it was clear that they were keen for me to take the lead in setting up some such organisation. I was initially reluctant to take on such a task. At diplomatic posts it can be easy to get too involved with one's own expatriates, with not enough time spent cultivating relationships with the local business and civic communities.

By being in at the beginning of a British business organisation in Houston I was in a position to write the rules, including some that I thought were essential to keep the organisation going on an active and effective basis. One such rule was to ensure that the presidency of the organisation circulated among the active British and American members and did not become the personal fief of one prominent member of the business community or of just a small group of resident British businessmen. Another rule was designed to make sure that the group did not have regular monthly meetings regardless of whether or not there was any particular purpose for any particular meeting. That is to say there should be general meetings only for specific purposes or when there was an interesting speaker available. The result of such rules was that it was easier to find good people to become office bearers and committee members.

I was also determined that the organisation should not turn into another social organisation, wasting time and energy on golf-meetings and such. There were many local clubs that expatriates could and should join for social and sporting 'networking' activities. By having meetings only when there was an interesting speaker it was possible to make it worthwhile for busy executives to attend.

One privilege I enjoyed as creator of the organisation was to give it a name; the name I put forward was 'British American Business Association', the initials forming the convenient acronym BABA. I did not explain to the founding members how I came to think of the name. Margaret and I were sitting at the marvellous open air opera theatre near Santa Fe, New Mexico where we were watching a performance of *The Rake's Progress*. I was fascinated by the character of the bearded lady, Baba the Turk, and decided that I would suggest the name BABA as the name for the business association in Houston. The name also made it clear that it was an organisation in which both American and British businessmen would participate on an equal basis, rather than being just a British business group to which Americans might belong. I was determined also that the organisation in Houston would not in any way be seen as, or thought to be, a branch of the British Chamber of Commerce in New York.

BABA turned out to be an extremely useful organisation. BABA had plenty of American as well as British members who played an equal and active part in the management of the association. Whenever a British minister or senior official, or any prominent British businessman who would be good value for an audience, visited Texas it was possible to arrange a BABA lunch-time meeting for a date that fitted in with the visitor's itinerary, rather than try and fit the speaker into a regular meeting date of the local group. For such visitors I had my core of a hundred people or so that I could count upon to turn up to hear the speaker.

Margaret and I were invited to Houston for the 25th Anniversary of what had at some time been renamed the 'British American Business Council'. I suspect that the word 'Association' tends to imply in the eyes of the United States Justice Department that the organisation concerned is a trade association having price fixing and other undesirable objectives. Sadly 'BABC' does not have the same tone to it as 'BABA', but it seems the organisation continued to grow and prosper in the years after Margaret and I left Texas.

An early project proposed to me locally as soon as I arrived in Houston was to organise a British Festival, to be held as one of a series sponsored by the American Institute of International Education. It did seem to be rather a case of catching the new arrival as soon as possible after he gets off the plane and inviting him to take on a project when he thinks the invitation to be flattering, and before he realises what is involved. I did agree to take on the task. Fortunately I had already learned certain things about the culture and working practices of the local business community, aspects that I might have easily overlooked. An early lesson was when Margaret and I attended the final grand event of a local German Festival, held soon after our arrival. That culmination of a week's hard and expensive work by my German colleague was held on a Thursday evening. I noticed that by 9 o'clock at the Festival Ball finale to the German week, even though the cultural performance provided by Germany was still in progress, local guests were streaming out of the banquet hall; those leaving early including among them some of the senior people from the major law firm who had invited Margaret and me to join their table as their guests.

I soon realised that the rather embarrassing early departures from an event over which a great deal of trouble had been taken and expense incurred, was because Houston business and professional people worked very long and hard. Business executives, lawyers and other professionals, especially those working in an international environment, all tended to arrive at their offices before 8 o'clock in the morning. That meant that from Mondays to Thursdays, no matter what the occasion, they went home promptly at 9 o'clock at night to get in a good night's sleep. They did not want to stay up partying until 11 or 12 on a weekday evening. That taught me that if we were going to have a British Festival it would have to be on condition that our main event was programmed to take place on a Friday night. On a Friday evening we might reasonably expect those attending to stay through the programme. The same experience taught me that to get busy local business people to a BABA or other committee meeting the thing to do was to schedule the meeting for no later than 8 o'clock in the morning – and to provide breakfast!

The next question was how did we finance the British Festival? The first answer as far as I was concerned was that it was no good going to London for financial support, so why even bother to ask? By the time we spent endless trouble and energy arguing with the London bureaucracy about how much was needed and what it was going to be used for, and which department would be responsible for providing any support, the event would be over! So we started off on the basis it was all going to be locally financed with the help of the Houston branch of the Institute of International Education and the local British community.

I viewed all activities of this kind as great opportunities for image building in the UK interest. But that meant that all the arrangements had to be first class in every respect. I was working to create a favourable image of Britain, and also of the local British business community. If cultural activity could be combined with some business aspect then so much the better. The Houston British Festival was an interesting experience of how to negotiate with people and explain to them what could be done, how one element in a programme would attract another. We ended up with a quite magnificent week of activity at no direct cost to the British taxpayer.

The central attraction for the British Festival came about as the result of a chance conversation at Houston airport when I met a member of the British community who had been an officer of the Welsh Guards. He suggested that I should ask the Band of the Welsh Guards if they would come to Houston for the week of the Festival. The Music Director of the Welsh Guards was keen, but explained that the band would need a $50,000 guarantee to cover all their travel expenses. This meant that I had to explain to the local office of the Institute of International Education, a non-profit organisation operating with support from the US government, that they would be required to put up a $50,000 guarantee for us to get the band as the centrepiece for what was really the IIE's British Festival.

Not surprisingly the American view was that the Welsh Guards would be just another military marching band. I had to work hard to explain to the local Director of IIE, the excellent Alice Pratt, that with the Welsh Guards the IIE would be getting not only a marching band but would also get a jazz band, a string orchestra, trios and quartets, and a 'big band' dance band for the final night; music for everything. The band would provide a whole week of varied entertainment.

Eventually the IIE agreed to underwrite the financial commitment. The Welsh Guards made the British Festival a tremendous success, to the extent that not only were all the Festival costs covered but the IIE received a financial contribution after meeting all the costs. Even I hadn't realised that in addition to the 'big band' music for the Festival Dinner, the audience would get a floor-show of counter-marching, which made a great impression on the audience. I remember one of the American guests at the top table asking me, 'Are they all actors?'

Once we had the presence of the Welsh Guards assured, we could attract something else. My wife and I had met George Thomas, the Speaker of the House of Commons, and were well aware of his love of anything to do with Wales and Welsh music. So my wife and I asked the Speaker of the House if he would like to come to the British Festival as the festival's

VIP visitor for the week and stay with us as a house guest for the nine days that the Welsh Guards were to be in Houston. He came, and during the week spoke to many audiences. He was, as so many know, a brilliant speaker. In Houston he was worth listening to whether he was talking to students, to the British American Business Association, or preaching at the principal Houston Methodist Church on Sunday: everybody found him a fascinating speaker. He gave a superb after-dinner speech at the big Festival Dinner that was the grand finale of British Week.

Attracting the Speaker of the House of Commons was not the end of it. Once it was known that George Thomas and the band of the Welsh Guards would attend, the marvellous Welsh singer and ex-member of the Goons, Sir Harry Secombe, said that he would like to come and sing with the Welsh Guards. With Harry Secombe coming to sing with the Welsh Guards, Tim Rice also came to play at the Festival dinner. They came at no cost to the Festival or to the British taxpayer.

So we had a spectacular British Festival Week with a most successful final event. I always set my objective for such projects as being to produce something that would be a hard act for my diplomatic colleagues to follow. The 1981 Houston British Festival certainly did a great deal to establish a higher profile for the presence of the British Consulate-General in the local community.

Apart from the local practice to start work early there was an aspect of Houston business culture that needed to be borne in mind when planning lunch-time talks for visitors. I had to impress upon the visitor that they must at all costs end their talk by 1.25 p.m. The Houston work ethic meant not only were all senior executives in their offices early in the mornings but they would all have appointments arranged for 2 p.m. in the afternoon. Whoever might be the speaker the audience would start to dissolve promptly at 1.30. Another characteristic was that hardly any Houston 'serious' business executives would drink at lunchtime and if they did it would be one glass of wine only. I had arrived in Houston believing in the legendary 'three martini lunch' only to discover very quickly that while that might happen in New York it certainly did not happen in Houston.

The *Economist* magazine made a mistake in not contacting me before they set out to make a big impression in Houston by arranging a lunch at which the speaker was to be a previous British Ambassador to Washington. If the ex-Ambassador had been a career diplomat matters might have been handled differently, but in this instance the featured speaker was a political 'family' appointee of the Labour Prime Minister Jim Callaghan. The *Economist* clearly thought they did not need any local official British advice on how to run a lunch speaker event.

I was invited to the lunch and was standing about talking with some oil executives that I knew personally when I began to realise that something was wrong. With time passing and no indication of a move into the dining-room, those with whom I was talking started to show irritation at being offered a second drink. The proceedings in the dining-room eventually started but some executive from the *Economist* was still making introductory remarks, including one or two feeble jokes, at 1.25 p.m. Guests started to sneak out before the guest speaker had even begun his address. All most embarrassing for the *Economist*, for the speaker, and to some extent for me as by then it had come to be assumed that I had something to do with every British 'manifestation' in Houston.

As Margaret and I began to know local 'society' certain characteristics became clear. When asked whether I liked Houston and Houstonians I would explain that people did not go to live in Houston because of the climate or the scenery. People went to Houston to make money; and when they had made money they wanted to be loved; and when they were loved they wanted to make sure they would be remembered – preferably in concrete: which is why Houston has such excellent museums, theatres, sports stadiums and so on, almost all of which have the names of principal donors attached to them.

Raising money for charity or the arts was in Houston primarily a matter of big fund-raising events. Such events would tend to be the field of a relatively small group of Houston business wives who would treat the matter as a challenge to do better and to raise more than each other. These fund-raising ladies were nonetheless all very supportive of each other's events. The support in its simplest form meant sponsoring, either in their own names or in the names of their husbands' businesses, one or more large tables at each other's fund-raising events. If you wanted to raise money in Houston success depended almost entirely on who had been persuaded to act at Chairman of the fund-raising campaign.

The English National Opera made a very costly mistake in this regard. I could have suggested two or three prominent socialite ladies in Houston who would have been delighted to accept responsibility for raising money for the visit to Texas by the ENO. What is more, whichever lady took on the task could have counted on strong support from all the other fund-raisers on the principle of mutual support over time. But without telling me, the ENO were persuaded by someone in London to nominate a 'rich Texan' well known in certain 'circles'. When I mentioned the name of Fossett to my fund-raising acquaintances the name was received with derision and comments to the effect that 'he hasn't lived in Texas for years'. Not many in the fund-raising circles of Houston in the 1980s were going to work to help an absentee Houstonian who had not supported any of their own local events for a long period. I fear that their choice for Chairman of the ENO support group for the Texas visit cost the ENO dearly.

The six States that comprised my 'Consular District' provided great variety. I have often said to people, and Americans agree with me, that there are many distinct cultures within those six States, including completely different ways of doing business. Even between Dallas and Houston there is a difference in the nature of local society and in the culture of doing business, let alone the more obvious differences between Houston and New Orleans, or between Houston, Denver and Oklahoma City, and of course Arkansas.

While I visited all other States in my territory quite frequently I made only one visit to Arkansas. There really wasn't any commercial activity in Arkansas that warranted further visits and it did seem to be a State where the population showed no significant interest in Ireland, the Falkland Islands or indeed Britain itself. Long after the event I worked out that my brief meeting with the Governor in Little Rock had been with Bill Clinton, recently re-elected as Governor of Arkansas. I have to admit that the extraordinary architecture of the Little Rock railway station made a more lasting impression on me than did the Governor.

Apart from keeping in touch with the oil and gas industry the four and a half years in Houston turned out for me personally to be more of a public relations job rather than being centred on trade matters. The issues of Northern Ireland hunger strikers and the Falklands War provided many opportunities to put the United Kingdom point of view, whether on radio talk shows, television appearances, or speeches whenever opportunity offered or could be secured by Helen Mann, the excellent Information Officer on my staff.

To make our mark throughout such a huge consular territory I made use of every opportunity that came my way. VIP visitors could be very useful in helping to gain a high profile. If a visitor was coming through any part of my territory, whether a government minister, prominent businessman or government official, I would endeavour to arrange a speaking engagement; not just to provide the visitor with an audience but to take the opportunity provided by the visit to spread the word for Britain and to spread the knowledge that I was the British Consul-General representing Britain in whichever State was being visited. Arranging such speaking occasions was also an effective way of steadily widening my range of personal contacts throughout the whole area. In arranging speaking engagements both in Houston and elsewhere, the branches of the English Speaking Union were always helpful, though some branches were much more effective than others. The ESU in Houston was particularly active and could be counted upon to produce an audience of two hundred for any significant British visitor.

Quite apart from the commercial and general representational activities one of the interesting aspects of work during the Houston posting was involvement with the media. In 1981 we had the problems of the Northern Ireland hunger strikers; in 1982 the Falkland Islands; and in 1983 the US military invasion of Grenada. These were all high profile issues attracting a lot of local attention throughout my area. It meant being very careful about what I said in public. I was in demand to speak or to appear on television at short notice to explain the British position on some recent development.

Whenever I travelled out of Houston Helen Mann, the Information Officer, would arrange for me to appear on local radio talk shows or make television appearances in whatever city I might be visiting. Whenever I was on a radio talk show for half an hour during the Northern Ireland problems, I would sit there knowing that sooner or later the Irish question would be raised by a caller; and it always did. The caller was invariably hostile towards the UK, but within minutes of the hostile question there would invariably be a follow-up call from a friendly listener. I believed that to represent the British position effectively, whether it was Northern Ireland or the Falkland Islands, it was essential always to answer questions positively and in a reasonable way.

I was invited to a television station in San Antonio for a panel discussion on the situation in Northern Ireland. The other members of the panel comprised some local personalities known to be rather unfriendly towards Britain in general and to Mrs Thatcher's government in particular. I prepared myself for a difficult time. The producer had assured our Information Officer that it was not intended to have a studio audience. Helen Mann had warned me not to take the producer's word, so I was quite prepared when, upon my arrival at the studio, I discovered – to the professed surprise of the producer – that there was indeed an audience and that the audience had been gathered together entirely from the local Irish community. Apart from one moment when I allowed my outrage at a particularly untruthful remark to get the better of my good temper, it went well. I like to think that I put the British point of view positively and 'diplomatically'. At least I did so so reasonably as to be applauded by the audience of Irish expatriates at the end of the programme, and for the leader of the Irish community to give me a lift back to the airport.

I learned always, whether in the Diplomatic Service or elsewhere, to adopt a practice of not responding to any single 'anti' report in the press – whatever the subject. The danger of reacting to every negative report is that what might well be a single comment that would otherwise be quickly forgotten by the public and the media, is given continued life, greater importance, and double the publicity, by the attention paid to the issue in the form of an immediate defensive response. In Houston, only if it became clear that a deliberate and perhaps co-ordinated campaign of bad publicity was getting under way would I set the Information Section to work to counter the adverse publicity and, if appropriate, arrange for me to deliver an answer to it.

On the other hand I accepted any invitation to speak in public or to talk to the media, believing it vital to respond to such invitations – you cannot run away from the difficult issues and leave the field open to the other side. I did really enjoy that part of my work. In my view the worst possible response to a question is 'no comment'. Journalists are trying to do the job they are paid for and it is always worthwhile giving them something to help them fulfil their task. If they cannot get some authoritative quote – even if it is a quote that really says nothing of substance – then they may have little alternative but to make something up. The problem with the printed press often lies, as I had learned from earlier experience, not with the journalists but with the sub-editor who makes up the headline: a headline that quite often proves to bear little relevance to the actual report that follows it.

*   *   *

The Falklands War was an issue of huge public interest throughout the USA, interest that was especially difficult to deal with from the Houston office. The problem for us in Houston was that our communications from London were not good. London was sending huge reams of classified material about the Falklands to the Embassy in Washington, but the Embassy had no time during the 'War' to put such confidential briefing material into a form that they could quickly pass on to a Consulate General where security facilities were of a lower grade. So I had to rely throughout on my own interpretation of the public news available.

At the time of the sinking of HMS *Sheffield*, a local TV station called to ask if I would go immediately to their studio and make a statement, 'live'. The TV station was about ten minutes away from the office. We were in a situation where I knew the disaster had happened – but we had no details whatever from official sources; nor for local technical reasons did we have access to television in the office. However, it happened that a recently retired member of my staff was at home that morning watching the news on her television set. She happened to be talking on the telephone to another member of the staff in the Consulate General telling her what she was seeing on television. She was seeing the latest ITN report of the incident.

The situation was that what was being said and shown on ITN in London, relayed to American television, was being called out to me across the office lobby as I walked out of the door of the Consulate-General to drive to the TV station. This meant that by the time I reached the television studio ten minutes later, I was almost as up-to-date as the local commentators who were themselves watching ITN on the studio's own television set. I had also had a few minutes to consider what I might say. In so far as last minute briefing was concerned that was more or less the situation I had to rely on for all the speaking that I undertook throughout the Falklands episode. I was in Oklahoma to talk to the English Speaking Union right at the height of the conflict, and I remember standing in the doorway of my hotel room closing it slowly as I watched CNN on my hotel room's television set, so that as I raced to the speaking engagement I would be as up to date as anyone in my audience.

One important aspect of speaking for Britain on difficult issues of the time, whether it be Northern Ireland, the Falklands, or indeed any subject of current international interest, was to maintain credibility. I have never hesitated to say that I consider my last eight years in the Diplomatic Service to have been an excellent time to be a British diplomat responsible for presenting the British view on contentious issues. That is to say that as far as I am concerned it was a very good time to be representing Britain while Mrs Thatcher was Prime Minister. This was not a matter of agreeing with every aspect of her policies. Personal agreement with a policy was in itself irrelevant to one's position as a career diplomat whose job it was to represent the British position whatever that position might be at the time. It was, as far as I am concerned, a good time to represent Britain because of Margaret Thatcher's consistency.

The Prime Minister's consistency meant that I could make a speech, I could appear on television, I could take part in a radio talk show, and I could then go to bed that night knowing that when I woke up in the morning the policy of the British government would still be the same. This meant that I could speak positively and in a confident manner, knowing that my official and personal credibility would be enhanced when it became obvious that my statements could be relied upon.

Credibility with one's audience, whether that audience might be a large group or just one or two senior officials of the host country, is an essential element in diplomacy. I am quite sure that many of my colleagues over the years, during the terms of previous governments, whether Labour or Conservative, had often felt that they would do well to hedge their remarks on public occasions just in case they woke up the next morning to find that the British government, of either political party, had suddenly modified its policy and made a fool of them. When Margaret Thatcher said, 'This Lady is not for turning,' it was useful to be able to take her at her word.

A diplomat must be both personally and officially credible. I remember one Houston acquaintance coming to me after the Argentineans had been defeated in the Falklands and saying, 'It happened exactly as you said it would.' Yet all I had done was little more than on numerous occasions emphatically to repeat the Prime Minister's statement that 'Either the Argentineans will leave peacefully or they will be made to go.' It was most important to be able to make such an unequivocal statement. Such a positive attitude went down well with American audiences. Indeed it was at times embarrassing that my Argentinean colleague had a much tougher time in his presentation.

With regard to local public relations aspects of the Falklands War guidance from London was that a Consul General could appear on the same television programme as his 'enemy' colleague but should not appear at the same time. This meant that when asked to join my Argentine colleague to discuss the Falklands on television, I could appear and say my piece either before or after my colleague; but we could not appear on screen together.

The Argentine Consul General in Houston at the time of the Falklands War had been a very friendly colleague before the invasion of the Falklands. When I met him on one television occasion to which we had each been invited to put our respective side of the argument, the TV producer decided to put me on first. When I came out of the studio after my ten minutes my Argentine colleague, waiting for his turn before the cameras. congratulated me for 'being a true gentleman' in the way I had put the British point of view. He then told me that his favourite posting had been seven years as Argentine Consul in Liverpool, and he introduced me to his 'British son'. His successor had also had the same experience of a long posting in Britain and told me that he had a British daughter. Unfortunately it was difficult for him, having newly arrived in Houston while the conflict was still proceeding, to develop a personal friendship with me. We were nonetheless always courteous towards each other when we met in the course of consular corps activity.

It can be most difficult for people who are personally good professional colleagues and friends but who find themselves on opposite sides of a contentious issue about which it is easy to become angry. The answer is that one doesn't have to be unpleasant about the colleague, one can make a good impression, perhaps a better one, without necessarily denigrating the other person and whatever he might have to say. I think the British position on the Falklands was quite well understood in my part of the United States – at least it was so after I had spent some months talking about it! The Grenada affair was a bit harder to explain to local audiences, but fortunately that was not as serious or as prolonged as the two other major issues of my time in Houston.

I stayed in Houston for four and a half years, about three and a half months longer than the standard posting to such a post. The reason was that towards the end of my stay in Houston, Margaret Thatcher, then at the height of her term as Prime Minister, was planning to make a visit to Texas. Because the visit would be to my territory, I as Consul-General, not the Ambassador, would be the one to 'host' a luncheon for the Prime Minister. I was asked if I would stay on for an extra three months to see the event through.

I had reached the stage of planning the luncheon for two hundred guests that I was to host in Dallas, and was wondering how on earth I was going to explain to many of our Houston friends that I could not possibly include them in the guest list. I could see my eventual departure from Houston being a little less friendly than it might have been. Then some unexpected bad news saved me. Something awful happened to the pound sterling exchange rate on the very day that Margaret Thatcher was planning to announce to Parliament her intended visit to Texas. The Prime Minister's visit was cancelled.

Margaret and I certainly enjoyed our time at Houston. We not only had a wonderful territory and plenty of opportunities to travel around it, we also made many good friends. We have taken a number of opportunities to revisit Houston in the years since we left. Some of the reasons we enjoyed our time there were the special visitors we had and the unusual number of stars of stage and screen that we met. Some of those encounters of an agreeable kind I will explain in the next chapter of this memoir.

CHAPTER 12

Encounters of a pleasant kind

I WAS AT TIMES TEMPTED TO TELL people that I stayed in the Diplomatic Service to keep my wife amused. Margaret certainly enjoyed certain aspects of our experiences and she certainly deserved some light relief from the living conditions in several of our posts. In a just world it would have been Margaret who received the decorations. I was just doing the job I was paid for but Margaret put up with a great deal that ordinary housewives certainly are not expected to have to tolerate, including one or two difficult ambassadors or their difficult wives. To make up for the difficult and uncomfortable times there were however many most agreeable encounters.

One wouldn't expect us to have met that many stars of stage and screen when we were in South Korea. I do not consider sitting at the opposite end of a table from Raquel Welch as counting. Yet in Seoul we did meet and spend time with Laurence Olivier, Margot Fonteyn and the principals of both the Royal Ballet and the Royal Opera. We also met the Australian icon Rolf Harris when Margaret and our children were asked to play a role as foreign tourists in an early promotional film being made by Pilgrim Films. In 1976 there were no European tourists visiting South Korea so the film was being made to start off a campaign for the beginnings of the South Korean tourist industry. Margaret and the children were to be filmed wandering through a re-created traditional Korean village. Rolf Harris was very friendly and Margaret and he got on well, as a photograph suggests.

The most opportunities for Margaret to meet some of her favourite stars came about while we were in Houston. We have a snapshot of Pavarotti with his arm around Margaret; and she has never forgiven me for failing to secure a copy of the photograph taken of her with Cary Grant, who kissed her twice on the same day. Then there was Larry Hagman, as well as meeting Greer Garson at the Greer Garson Theatre in Santa Fe – and what a beautiful and charming person she was. My turn came with a meeting with Shirley MacLaine.

Lynn Wyatt, definitely one of Houston's expert hostesses who really entertained in elegance, gave a private party for Sam Wanamaker at the Wyatts' home on River Oaks Boulevard. Sam Wanamaker was on a fundraising tour in aid of his Globe Theatre project. Guests at the party included Shirley MacLaine who was in Houston filming *Terms of Endearment*. Cleo Laine and her husband John Dankworth, Michael York, and others from the world of screen and stage were also guests at a party for about thirty in all. We were all enjoying pre-dinner drinks when Lynn came up to me and said, 'Richard, the paparazzi are still here and they won't leave until they have got some photographs of Shirley; would you stand in the corner and talk to Shirley while they take photographs. The photographers will then leave and we can all enjoy dinner.'

So I went into a corner of the room to stand and talk with Shirley MacLaine We talked and we talked, and were still talking when the photographers had left. The next morning Betty Ewing, then the Social Editor for the *Houston Chronicle*, telephoned me and asked, 'Richard, what were you talking to Shirley Maclaine about for all that time?'

I was able to be absolutely honest and reply, 'Australian politics.' Although I was in Houston as British Consul General, Shirley had heard that I had Australian connections. What she wanted to know was what I thought were the prospects for Andrew Peacock making a political come-back in Australia. Andrew Peacock's early brilliant political career had suffered a set-back for reasons I do not recall. What I did recall when Shirley MacLaine mentioned his name was that there had been rumours, based on something she had written in one of her autobiographies, that she had had a close friendship with a young politician. Some speculators thought the object of her interest had been a British Labour Party politician. I immediately guessed however that it was Andrew Peacock who had a special place in Shirley's pantheon of friends and admirers. So I was able without pause to make all the right remarks about a 'young politician for whom there was still plenty of time to resume a successful and prominent career etcetera, etcetera . . .'. Andrew Peacock did indeed make a comeback, not as a politician so much as being appointed by the Prime Minister of the day to be Australian Ambassador to Washington. It is easy to guess whose name immediately began to appear in the published guest lists for receptions at the Australian Embassy. I do have a very nice photograph to remind me of that conversation with Shirley, yet another pleasant and beautiful person met as a fringe benefit of a diplomat career.

Beside film stars there were also other notable meetings. I suspect Margaret and I have met more Presidents of the United States than most Americans ever meet. We met President Carter, Mrs Carter and Amy, in Seoul. When he was campaigning for election Jimmy Carter said that if elected he would 'bring our boys home from Korea'. I have always admired him for changing his mind within a month of becoming President. The American military presence on the Korean peninsula has been the most successful peace-keeping operation ever. Without having any evidence to prove it, I have always maintained that I would not be surprised if it was the Japanese, the Chinese and the Soviets who persuaded Carter to change his mind. The Korean peninsula has been described as 'a dagger pointed at the heart of Japan' or as 'the bridge to Manchuria'. Unifying North and South Korea would be rather like pulling the plug out of a bath full of water: no one in the neighbourhood could be sure which way things might move. A unified peninsula could be a worrying problem for any or all of its three neighbours. It could yet be the site for the beginning of another war in our time.

The Carters came to Seoul as a Head of State accompanied by his family. Protocol required that as Head of State he should be greeted by the whole Seoul Diplomatic Corps, or to be accurate perhaps by all those members of the corps who represented countries with which the USA had diplomatic relations. As Mrs Carter was accompanying her husband, the wives of resident diplomats were also expected to turn up to welcome the visitors. I was British Chargé d'Affaires at the time so Margaret and I were invited to join all the Ambassadors and other Chargés at the location of an emergency air strip built on a wide new highway quite close to the centre of the city. As I was a very junior Chargé in the context of Diplomatic Corps protocol, Margaret and I were placed at the very end of the long line of some fifty diplomats standing waiting for twenty minutes or more for the President and Mrs Carter to arrive.

Looking behind us Margaret noticed a bored little girl sitting on some steps and being watched over by two tall and well-built American guards immediately identifiable as being from the presidential Secret Service security detail. Margaret went over to chat with Amy. Amy was indeed bored and told Margaret that she would much rather be at the hotel swimming pool. After they had been talking for some time we received advice that the President was about to arrive. Margaret rejoined me in the line-up and Amy was led off to join her mother and father as her parents were taken to the head of the long diplomatic queue. After a brief conversation with the Dean of the Diplomatic Corps and the American

Ambassador, the Carters set off down the length of the long line, quickly shaking hands with each Ambassador and moving on to the next one, until they got to us at the 'junior' end of the diplomatic corps. Amy immediately showed that she was pleased at last to see in Margaret someone she actually recognised; so Amy, the President and Amy's mother stopped to talk to us for several minutes. Our friends and colleagues watching the proceedings on television, and some of my diplomatic colleagues higher up the seniority list and much higher up the greeting line, later wanted to know: 'Why did the President stop and talk to you for so long?' I let my colleagues assume that it was due to the 'special relationship' between the USA and the UK.

Of presidential encounters while I was Consul-General in Houston my brief encounter with Clinton, then Governor in Little Rock, hardly counts. On the other hand we did spend a little time with Vice President George Bush and his very likeable wife Barbara. We met them when Barbara Bush launched the nuclear submarine USS *Houston* at Norfolk, Virginia. The Houston-based conglomerate that owned the naval shipbuilding yard invited us to the ceremony and the associated overnight entertainment in Williamsburg. The launch did not go absolutely according to plan. There was a strong wind blowing across the bow of the ship and the Vice-President's wife swung the champagne bottle twice without it breaking. An Admiral stepped forward to help Mrs Bush swing the bottle a third time. The launch then went ahead successfully.

Barbara Bush was a delightful, almost motherly, person to meet and we came away most impressed with both her and her husband. I would afterwards tell Americans that we 'as foreigners' thought George Bush and Barbara were definitely presidential material with whom the international community would be happy. Foreign governments felt he understood the world; but at the same time I said that I realised that the American voters might not see George Bush in quite the same way. A pity that while his international reputation was so good his neglect of domestic matters and domestic politics led to him missing a second term.

I met the Vice-President again at a small private drinks party in Houston. Margaret was invited also but the number that could attend the occasion was strictly limited. Margaret did the decent thing and gave up her place on the guest list so that our house-guest at the time, George Thomas, Speaker of the House of Commons, could attend in her place. The nearest I ever got to George Bush after that was when he was President, some years after I had left the Diplomatic Service and I was doing something that was if anything even more international than my diplomatic career. I was invited by one of the presidential advisors to have lunch with him in the Executive Dining Room at the White House. It was on a Thursday, and because George Bush liked Mexican food the menu was always Tex-Mex on Thursdays during his time in the White House. It was all very informal and my host and I were seated at a table next to the President's table. Unfortunately I ate too fast. We left the dining room before the President himself arrived.

We met Gerald Ford at the University of Texas at Austin. Margaret and I were attending a symposium held to mark the 50th Anniversary of FDR's first election as President. Margaret did not find Ford a particular scintillating personality and the occasion was more notable for meeting Lady Bird Johnson, widow of LBJ. Lady Bird is someone who will be remembered for the many good things she did in Texas, especially her campaign to plant thick banks of 'blue bonnets' and 'Indian paint brushes' along the edges of Texas highways. Margaret and Lady Bird got on well together. What a pleasant and much respected person she was. I was present at the event in Austin to deliver a message from The Queen Mother, a task that was in itself a nice sequel to the individual separate experiences Margaret and I had each had of being in the presence of The Queen Mother many years earlier.

The University of Texas at Austin had the correct idea of how to go about extending an invitation to The Queen Mother. They did not write to the Palace, and they did not write to the Embassy in Washington. If they had attempted either of those channels the request would have been referred straight back to me for comment and advice in my capacity as HM Consul General for the State of Texas. I might have been a little put out that such a prestigious Texas institution should have thought they could ignore me. Instead the letter came directly to me in Houston.

The organisers of the symposium referred to the friendship that King George VI and Queen Elizabeth enjoyed with the Roosevelts, especially during the years of World War 2. The letter writers asked if I would on their behalf convey to Her Majesty The Queen Mother an invitation to attend the symposium and deliver a message to mark the 50th anniversary of FDR's first election as President. I certainly was not going to recommend that The Queen Mother travel all the way to Texas just to deliver a message to the symposium. But in my letter to Clarence House I said that Her Majesty might wish to consider sending a message that I could read out on her behalf. I did not leave it for her staff at Clarence House to start from scratch to think about what might be an appropriate message. To make it easy I added, 'Perhaps along the lines of the attached draft.' It was most pleasant to receive a reply to the effect that: 'Her Majesty would be pleased if you would on her behalf read the message exactly as you have written it.'

The most agreeable meetings we have ever had were certainly the series of visits by members of The Royal Family. During my four and a half years as Consul General at Houston I had responsibility for a total of nine visits by six different members of the Royal Family. In formal terms I had responsibility for a member of the Royal Family from the moment they landed in my territory until they boarded the plane to fly onwards. On a few of the visits I was not responsible for drawing up the detailed programme. If anything with a visit went awry it was on such visits, not on the visits for which I did the detailed planning. I spent many evening hours working out details of each programme.

There is needless to say a correct method of referring to particular members of the Royal Family, something that tends to be a mystery to most British people let alone to Americans. In some ways it doesn't really matter for general purposes whether one needs to explain the difference between the titles: 'Her Royal Highness The Princess Margaret', 'Her Royal Highness Princess Alexandra' and 'Princess Michael of Kent'; so I shall take the liberty of referring to them in more simple terms when writing of their visits with which we were involved. Sufficient for me to take the liberty of recording that our experiences made it clear that they all work hard in their different ways; that they were the most valuable support to my work in 'promoting Britain'; and they were all most agreeable and helpful to us. We have nine autographed photographs, our problem being that we do not have room for a grand piano on which to display them.

Our experiences made us both firm admirers of all six of the 'Royals' for whom we had the privilege of making certain that their visits went well. I tried to make sure the arrangements were such as to make a visit agreeable for both the visitors and the local people who were involved in the separate programmes. There were occasions when a visitor had every reason to be a little terse as things went wrong. That certainly applied to HRH The Duke of Edinburgh on his visit to Houston arranged by and for the World Wildlife Fund. One item in the programme was a visit to a local bird reserve in wetlands not far from Houston. On a very hot and humid Houston summer afternoon the party paddled about in canoes on a semi-swamp, seeing not a single bird. The birds weren't stupid. The birds were all resting while sheltering from the unpleasant climate. Only mad dogs etcetera . . . go out in the mid-day heat and humidity of the southern Texas coastal wetlands.

On the evening of the same day as the uncomfortable and sweaty visit to the swamp, Prince Philip was scheduled to speak at a typical Houston fund-raising dinner. The dinner was a sell-out as such events often are in Houston if the organisation seeking to raise money goes about it in a way that suits the local culture. The eating part of the dinner went smoothly and in due course the Royal patron of WWF rose to speak. I was sitting at the top table five or six along from the guest of honour so it was probably just as well I could not see the expression on his face when he started to speak. The huge hotel ballroom was divided into three sections. The tables in two of the sections were all quiet and waiting politely to hear what the Duke had to say. But one-third of the room went on chattering loudly and taking not the slightest notice. The organisers had not made sure that all the audio system was working properly. I think His Royal Highness would have been entirely justified in being a little terse with those who had asked him to travel all the way to Houston to deliver a carefully prepared speech in support of the World Wildlife Fund's cause only to deliver the speech to a noisy crowd.

My first Royal visitor was Princess Margaret who came to Houston to open an exhibition of The Queen's collection of Leonardo da Vinci drawings. I went to the airport to meet her and waited at the end of the passenger bridge to the aircraft. I shall never forget that when the door of the British Caledonian Airways VC10 opened, there framed in the doorway of the aircraft I saw a very pretty petite woman. It was a delightful and memorable first impression.

It was on Princess Margaret's first visit to Texas during my time as Consul General that Margaret and I met and later became good friends with Lynn Wyatt. The visit had been arranged with the local museum long before I arrived in Houston. The Princess and Lynn Wyatt had become acquainted in London and the Princess stayed during the visit at the Wyatts' home. Among the social events to which we were invited was a dinner party for sixteen in the 'Wine Cellar at Tony's', at the time a most fashionable eating house – one to which socially aspiring Houstonians would go to see and be seen rather than because of the food. It was situated in a very ordinary shopping precinct close to the famous Galleria Mall. The Wine Cellar was really no more than an artificial creation that provided a sophisticated atmosphere quite out of keeping with the very ordinary external appearance of the building.

When Princess Margaret was planning a second visit to Texas, this time to Dallas to open a British fair at Nieman Marcus, I was in the position of needing to put together a programme that included some relaxation. By then I had such confidence in Lynn Wyatt's abilities as a hostess that I asked her if she would organise a dinner in the Wine Cellar at The Mansion on Turtle Creek in Dallas. By that time Princess Margaret and her staff probably had some confidence that I as Consul General would not make a mess of the arrangements for her visit.

I had apparently established something of a reputation with London at the time of the earlier visit when Princess Margaret and her party went on from Houston to New Orleans for a brief stay before travelling to Mustique. On all later visits by Royal visitors to New Orleans I made it my practice to accompany the visiting party throughout their time in my territory but on this first occasion, before I had honed my skills in arranging such visits, I had left the Princess and her party in the safe hands of our excellent Honorary Consul in New Orleans, Jimmy Coleman. Jimmy was the ideal person to entertain VIP visitors. He was very good at it and knew everyone that mattered in his city. He was also able on this occasion to accommodate the visiting party in his family's home in the Garden District. On the day before his house guest was due to move on, he telephoned to me in some alarm. Princess Margaret was not feeling well and it was thought she would not be able to cope with the commercial flight from New Orleans to Miami to be followed by another two flights on to Mustique. Jimmy had other commitments for the use of his home as well as for his business and he did not quite know how to arrange for his house guest and her party to proceed with their journey. I told Jimmy to leave the problem with me.

Fortunately by the time this minor crisis developed I had already made friends with senior executives of a number of oil companies, each of which I knew had several corporate aircraft at their disposal. I was able to call the President of a company in Dallas and ask whether he might be able to help me by flying Princess Margaret to Miami to enable her at least to avoid the hassle of the commercial flight for that leg of her onward journey. Without any hesitation my friend said that he would be happy to arrange for the party to be flown directly to the Carribbean. I was able to call our Honorary Consul back and tell him he could advise his guests that I had arranged for a BAC111 jet to be available to carry the party for almost the whole of their journey to Mustique.

The next visit was a lengthy and most memorable visit by Princess Anne. She had accepted an invitation to open a British Fair at an 'British' primary school in Denver.

The visit was then extended by a visit for three days to New Mexico and two days in Houston. There were many agreeable incidents in that visit, a visit for which I became responsible for organising the programme apart from the actual formalities connected with the school fair.

The Rockies west of Denver are beautiful at any time of year and there is much to see within reasonable reach of Denver, so we paid a couple of visits into the mountains sightseeing and to have lunch with Governor Richard Lamm and his wife at the historic George Town. I found out that when being driven about the one thing our visitors did not want was the noise and fuss of police motor-cycle escorts. Such noisy escorts, together with the associated blocking of crossroads, serve only to annoy the local drivers and are thus not good public relations for the visitor. So we managed always with just an unmarked car or two carrying security personnel.

It was left to the Secret Service detail to arrange how they shared responsibility for the security arrangements between themselves and the local police. The local police were always keen to show off their motor-cycle escort capabilities and it required some diplomacy on the part of the Secret Service personnel to make sure things went as our visitors wished. When we accompanied Princess Anne to visit the secret under-ground headquarters of NORAD in Cheyenne Mountain it was explained to me that the forty-five minute drive from Denver to Colorado Springs involved passing through the territories of seven different police forces. This meant that there had to be negotiations with all seven police authorities as to arrangements for the passage of the visiting party's convoy of just four unmarked cars. The agent told me that the smaller the police force the more difficult they were to deal with. The Chief of Police of any suburban force did not like being denied an opportunity to show off.

Towards the end of the visit to Denver I received a message from the lady-in-waiting to the effect that Princess Anne would like me to organise a small dinner party for her to thank those who had extended private hospitality to her. The easiest arrangement I could make would be simply to go to the Brown Palace Hotel, with its connections to the Unsinkable Molly Brown of *Titanic* fame. I could simply hire a private room at the historic hotel and no one would question the choice. But it would have been just another hotel dining room and another hotel menu. Being reckless I decided it would be much more fun and interesting for the visitor if I organised the dinner for fourteen at the Buckhorn Exchange, down by the railroad tracks.

The Buckhorn Exchange was a genuine old restaurant getting its name from its early role as a place where railroad workers could cash their wage cheques. It was full of genuine Western memorabilia. It transpired that none of the guests from Denver 'society' had ever been to the Buckhorn Exchange and some of them were a little uncertain about driving into that part of town for any purpose whatever. Having myself been to the restaurant before, and after conducting a quick reconnaissance, it was clear that there was an alcove that would allow the hostess to sit at the head of the table where she could not be seen from the main body of the restaurant. I would sit at the other end of the table which would be visible to the public. Two tables for four, situated just outside the entrance to the alcove, would provide discreet seating for the security detail who could dine at the same time as the main party. It all worked very well. The only embarrassing moment was when one of the visiting party asked for an explanation of what exactly were the 'prairie oysters' featured on the restaurant menu. I was told twenty-five years after the dinner that the photograph taken while I was pointing out to Princess Anne the legendary prairie 'jackaloupe' sitting in a glass cabinet among other 'Western' artefacts, was still on the wall of the restaurant.

The only other near embarrassment during the visit was at the Sunday morning church service in the large Episcopalian church in Denver. I had undertaken a careful reconnaissance of the space at which I was to read a Lesson while standing at a lectern placed next to a large pillar. What I hadn't allowed for was that the church was so packed that an additional chair had been added to the row next to the lectern. When I came to read the Lesson I had to squeeze in to stand with one foot raised and supported by the base of the pillar. Within a few seconds of standing there my left leg began to tremble with the trembling getting more violent as the reading progressed. I was lucky to get to the end without having to make some violent movement to rescue my left leg.

From Denver we went on to Santa Fe, New Mexico, where I had arranged for the party to stay at the Rancho Encantado, a typical but quite modest Western style resort for people who wanted to ride into the hills in the spectacular area around it. The resort was particularly notable for being the creation of Betty Egan who had been decorated with an MBE for heroic services during World War 2. Not surprisingly some horse-riding was in the programme with an evening barbecue in the hills behind the resort. It was the first time either Margaret or I had been on a horse of any kind for many years. Fortunately Princess Anne went off well ahead and left us behind dealing with the problem that the horse Margaret was riding did not want to move at all. Nonetheless, after negotiating some quite tricky mountain tracks we made it to the barbecue site and very pleasant it was too. Margaret decided she would ride back to the ranch in one of the available jeeps but I thought I would risk it by staying with my trusty steed. I then learnt what it is like to be a cowboy sliding down a steep sand dune with his horse on its haunches. Fortunately I had picked up the tip of how to lean back in the saddle. It was a spectacular experience, riding down from the hills as the sun set slowly in the west and the stars came out across the cloudless sky; rather like a romantic Roy Rogers Western – with only soft guitar music missing.

The next day we went into the Taos Pueblo to meet the Taos people. The programme began with the visitors seated with the Chief and other seniors of the tribe in a wide half-circle twenty metres or so from the totem pole while the tribal women danced in traditional manner around the pole. This all seemed harmless enough, but after a little while I realised that the Chief's wife had left the group at the totem pole and was walking towards Princess Anne, seated ten or twelve places to one side of where Margaret and I were sitting. I guessed that the Princess was about to be invited to join the women going round the totem pole, an item not in the programme. I had no idea how Princess Anne would react. I need not have worried. Princess Anne and her lady-in-waiting promptly joined the group and a few minutes later we were all going round the totem pole. To say the visitors were 'dancing' round the totem pole might be an exaggeration: 'shuffling around in the sand' would be a more accurate description as I remember it. There was not a single photographer present and the visit was well before the time of mobile-phone cameras.

After the totem pole event we all moved to join the long line of cars to take us to lunch. I had worked out exactly which of the party would be in which car; so I was rather put out when instead of getting into the allocated limousine I saw Princess Anne being directed into a battered old blue sedan. I said aloud, but more or less to myself, 'Oh. Oh. That's not in the programme.' A New Mexico State Police officer standing close enough to hear me said, 'You're in Indian Territory now.' He explained to me that the State Police were allowed into the Taos reserve only if invited, even if the purpose of the visit was to pursue a member of the tribe who was suspected of committing a crime outside the reserve. Another matter the tribe can control is access by the media.

We had a very good lunch of local food. A large table had been set up under a plastic awning and the food was served from a variety of large bowls. When it came to a few formal remarks of welcome both the Chief and the Casique spoke. I gained the impression that the Casique, the 'Witch doctor' of the tribe, was really a more powerful figure in their society than the Chief. The whole experience was a privilege and left me with a very good impression of the Taos community and its strong determination to preserve its traditional society and its traditional values. I shall be disappointed if I am told that the Taos people now operate a casino as so many other tribes have done in pursuit of the almighty dollar.

There were a couple of brief formal calls in Santa Fe and a visit to the Greer Garson Theatre with 'Mrs Minerva' herself present to greet the visitor. And what a beautiful and charming person was Greer Garson, by then in her early 80s.

From Santa Fe the party flew to Houston for two days before Princess Anne went on to New Orleans and then returned to London. It was in Houston that we had the opportunity to present to her the three of our four children then living 'at home'. Princess Anne demonstrated an easy ability to make young people relax in her presence. By the time I saw her off on her way back to London Margaret and I had become firm admirers of someone who could be counted upon to take a visit seriously and yet be so pleasant and considerate to us and anyone else who contributed to her visit.

In New Orleans Honorary Consul Jimmy Coleman could be counted upon to arrange any event superbly, but I had a few bad minutes accompanying Princess Anne just before we reached Preservation Hall. I was very keen for our visitor to visit Preservation Hall for a few minutes to hear elderly musicians who played jazz without having their music spoilt by any form of electronic amplification. We were a little ahead of the time that Jimmy Coleman had arranged for our group to be able to enter Preservation Hall without waiting in line. As we approached our destination Jimmy said something to the effect that 'We are early. Let's go in here for a few minutes and have a drink.' I suddenly realised we were walking into Murphy's Irish Bar: definitely not in the programme. If I had been asked I would at a time of Northern Ireland problems have put any suggestion of visiting any establishment with such a name as definitely in the 'over my dead body' category. In the event of the slightest hint of unpleasantness I could see it being a case of 'What did you think you were doing taking Her Royal Highness into an Irish Bar?' For all I knew Murphy's could have been the drinking hole for the local IRA supporters. As it happened, nothing happened, and we went on to Preservation Hall some ten minutes later. After Preservation Hall what else could we possibly do but have dinner at Antoine's. New Orleans was of course a star in my territory. Margaret and I became very fond of the city. I think of the ultimate day in New Orleans as being breakfast at Brennan's; lunch at Commander's Palace; dinner at Antoine's; with late night coffee and beignets at Café du Monde. If ever there was an urban area with atmosphere, it has to be the French Quarter. The irony is I suppose that New Orleans would not have the French Quarter if the city had prospered in the fifty years after the Civil War.

Princess Anne returned to my territory the following year to support fund-raising efforts for the British Olympic team in advance of the 1984 Los Angeles Games. We were delighted to have another opportunity to be able to arrange a programme for someone we had come to admire greatly. The initial planning for the second visit gave rise to something that made me wonder about just how sure members of the Royal Family can be about the advice they get from 'courtiers' and 'friends'. I received a message to the effect that one of the Princess's friends had suggested she would enjoy a visit to Gillies Bar, an establishment that had installed one of the first mechanical bucking broncos. 'Over my dead body' was my immediate reaction. I knew of Gillies Bar but felt that I could not be so emphatic in condemning the very idea of a visit to it unless I had actually been to the place myself. So I got in my car and drove to the location on the highway between Houston and Galveston. It was a huge area of 'traditional Western' beer hall. I bought myself a beer and observed the mechanical monster. I returned to Houston and the next day sent a message very much to the effect of 'over my dead body'. It would have been a disaster whatever did happen or did not happen on such a visit. The media would have had a field day just by knowing she might visit the bar, and would have been able to generate publicity of the unpleasant kind just as much if she declined to ride the bucking bronco as if she did ride it. I have always wondered whether whoever suggested the idea in the first place was treacherous or simply foolish.

While we were in Houston The Prince of Wales came to my consular territory for a visit to New Mexico. The purpose of the visit was to open a campus of the World College in which The Prince of Wales had shown interest over a long period. Armand Hammer, of Occidental Petroleum, was the sponsor of the New Mexico branch of the college. For the purpose, an old hotel building dating from the railway boom of the nineteenth century was taken over. The structure was of the grand 'castle' type favoured by north American railroads hoping to attract passengers for their trans-continental routes. The location was generally referred to as the 'Castle at Montezuma'. It was a grand concept on a very short but now defunct branch line from the main line of the railroad. I gather that the Aitcheson, Topeka and Santa Fe Railroad never actually passed through Santa Fe. I have also since discovered that not many people who live in New Mexico seem to have any idea where Montezuma is or even to have heard of it.

One of the problems to be faced in planning for the visit was to find accommodation for those members of the Prince's entourage who could not be accommodated in the buildings of the 'castle' complex. On a reconnaissance Margaret and I discovered one motel within a workable distance of the college site. It happened to be on Route 66 at a point between Amarillo and Santa Fe. The building was typical of so many highway motels depicted on American television. This one was however slightly unusual in that it was built with every unit looking on to an inner compound, with just one narrow vehicle entrance and exit. The first impression on us was that perhaps the structure was meant to imaginatively recreate the 'circling of the wagons' atmosphere of its remote location in cowboy and Indian territory. That romantic illusion was dissolved and the quality of the usual clientele clearly indicated when we asked the proprietor's wife why none of the rooms had windows on the sides that overlooked the remarkable local scenery. Her reply was to the effect that if they had put windows on the side of the unit rooms that looked outwards, then the television sets and anything else moveable in a room would have disappeared through the windows overnight. The design of the building was intended to make sure that the owners might see what was being carried out in departing tenants' cars when they had to pass the motel office window on their way back to the highway. So much for the 'romance' of Route 66.

The visit to open the World College at Montezuma, New Mexico provided examples of how the Royal Family may from time to time receive bad advice, and where it can be useful to have someone resident in the area to be visited and who can perhaps help avoid public relations disasters. At the early stages of the planning for the visit by The Prince of Wales, London told the Embassy that Prince Charles had agreed to give an exclusive interview to Barbara Walters, one of the three powerful ladies of American television. The Information Section of the Embassy had correctly reacted along the lines that if he gave one of the three women an exclusive interview the other two could be counted upon to rubbish the Prince's visit. The solution was to give an 'exclusive' interview to each of the three. I do not know how Barbara Walters reacted to the idea but it was a solution that worked well.

A room in the Montezuma Castle was set up as a studio. The first fifteen-minute interview was with Barbara Walters. While that interview was in progress the two other interviewers were kept in a side-room where they could neither hear no see the first interview. Then the second interview took place while the third interviewer remained in isolation. The Prince dealt with all three interviews perfectly, including neatly putting down the third interviewer when she asked a foolish question asking what he dreamt about.

Margaret met one or her favourite film stars at the opening ceremony of the College. We were seated in the front row of the audience and at the end of the ceremonies we stood ready to leave. Margaret turned around to look at the audience and immediately recognised someone even though she had not previously met him. Without thinking she pointed to him, saying, 'It's you!' The object of this attention gestured back, 'Yes. It's me.' Margaret then beckoned to him, summoning him to come to meet her. It was Cary Grant. It made Margaret's day. We talked to him again that evening at a small reception to mark the occasion and ever since Margaret has been able to say that she was kissed by Cary Grant twice on the same day. He was yet another famous person who was a delight to meet, as was his wife: his sixth wife I think. Cary Grant was then over eighty but still as handsome as his wife was beautiful.

The second problem with the plans for the visit to New Mexico by The Prince of Wales was that the initial programme had been drawn up with only the Armand Hammer interest in the World College in mind. Once the opening of the World College had been opened it was intended that all the guests present at the opening ceremony would be transported from Montezuma to Albuquerque. At Albuquerque, the largest city in New Mexico, the guests from Montezuma would be joined by many others at a grand fundraising function. It was perhaps not surprising that the *amour propre* of the ordinary citizens of New Mexico had been overlooked; there would be little if any money to be raised from a visit to the much smaller State capital, Santa Fe. I made a strong protest to the effect that if the heir to the British Throne on his very first visit to the State of New Mexico ignored the State capital and the State Governor, then we could expect some very adverse comments in the local press. To ignore the State capital, only an hour's drive from Albuquerque, would correctly be seen as a discourteous snub to the State and its inhabitants, including the State's Indian tribes.

The difficulty was how to adjust the programme and deal with complicated logistics for getting the Prince of Wales to Santa Fe and on to the fund-raiser. The solution was for the main party to travel from Montezuma to Albuquerque as planned. Prince Charles, Lord Romsey, Margaret and I, plus the Prince's detective, would fly to Santa Fe from a rural airport near Montezuma, doing so in a small Occidental corporate aircraft arranged by Armand Hammer. In Santa Fe we would spend an hour or so calling on the Governor and attending a small welcoming ceremony before going on by road to the big fund-raiser in Albuquerque. It worked. The Prince was well received. As in our earlier experience when Princess Anne visited the Taos pueblo, there was however an unexpected item in the programme. On this occasion, fortunately, the Prince was not expected to dance around a totem pole but instead to accept and have placed on his head a full Indian feathered head-dress. It all went well.

The reception at Albuquerque was for a thousand people. The dress code was 'black tie and flash camera'. The Prince's detective and I endeavoured to clear a way for the guest of honour as he slowly worked his way through the throng while the flash cameras went off almost continuously. One lady asked me, 'What does he talk about? He seems to have something to say to everyone.' He did indeed: a skill few of us possess. When the Prince had completed the circuit we paused briefly for a drink and I then accompanied him to the airport for his onward flight taking him out of my area of responsibility. Another most agreeable experience concluded. While I went to the airport to see Prince Charles on his way, Margaret and the other guests sat down to dinner. I caught up with them later.

Princess Alexandra paid two visits while I was in Houston. The first one was to Denver, when she was accompanied by her husband Sir Angus Ogilvie: two more delightful people it was a privilege to be with in my official capacity. For their visit to Colorado I arranged an informal picnic for six at a public picnic table in a mountain park above beautiful Lake Echo not far from Denver. I had had an opportunity to view the location on an earlier visit. The picnic was arranged for a weekday so I was confident there would be few if any members of the public about. A young local executive from Sir Angus Ogilvie's company went ahead with his wife, picked out a table under the trees about fifty metres from the roadway, set up the table for lunch and then waved us down as we approached. There was just one security car and that stayed parked on the road out of sight of the wooden table where six of us had an undisturbed lunch in the quiet forest with some snow still on the ground around the table.

Prince and Princess Michael of Kent came to my area on two occasions to assist with charity fund-raising events, once to Houston and once to Dallas. As with all our other visitors to Houston the Kents were pleasant people with whom to spend time. Prince Michael delivered a particularly good speech at a lunch at The Mansion on Turtle Creek in Dallas. Margaret however remembers that event most for the fact that it was there that she met Larry Hagman who, like many of us, Margaret identified with his role as J. R. Ewing in *Dallas* as much as for his earlier role in the TV series *I Dream of Jeannie*.

Altogether our four and a half years in Houston were most agreeable. I am often asked to indicate which of our diplomatic postings we liked best. I answer that they were all different. Brasilia was an unusual first posting that provided the need and opportunity to learn to speak Portuguese and to see the interior of a country that has huge potential. It is always good to be 'in charge'. Phnom Penh was certainly the most exciting but also the saddest.

Seoul was the most rewarding from a job satisfaction point of view for anyone interested in international trade. Houston was the most agreeable, not least because three of our four children were able to live with us for most of the time we were there. Roger gained an MBA at Rice University, and Peter a BBA at University of Houston, while Sarah became something of an expert selling opals in the Galleria. Their time in Houston set them all up for independent lives later. Our second daughter missed out on the Texas experience because she had decided to stay in Australia and get married. After Houston came Hanoi, completing my experience of countries that live in the shadow of China and providing lessons and experiences that were new and as fascinating as anything that we had had before.

With ny new posting came advice that I had been promoted to the Senior Grade in HM Diplomatic Service.

CHAPTER 13

Hanoi: 1985–87

APPOINTMENT AS ONE OF HER MAJESTY'S Ambassadors was certainly something worth working towards and that much more rewarding for being a career achievement rather than being a political appointment or, as sometimes seems to be the case with American ambassadors, an appointment based on the size of the donation made to a presidential campaign. While modern communications have resulted in ambassadors having rather less influence or discretion than in the past, there remains, especially in more distant lands, considerable value in having as a nation's representative an individual who has had years of experience and who may have an understanding of the local culture and economy.

One of the great experiences that Margaret and I shared was being received at Buckingham Palace, as *The Times* reported in the Court Circular of the day, for the ceremony of 'kissing of hands' on my appointment as Her Majesty's Ambassador to Vietnam. No doubt in the interests of hygiene the practice of actually kissing the hand of the monarch was dropped a long time ago; but the ceremony of being summoned to Buckingham Palace and for Margaret to have 'the honour of being received' was certainly special indeed. Margaret and I sat with The Queen for half an hour with no other person present in the room. We discussed Vietnam for some time and I began to think that Margaret was not going to say a word: most unlike her. But Margaret reminded me afterwards that she had been brought up not to speak until spoken to when in the presence of even Vice-Regal personages, let alone in the presence of The Queen. After some little while The Queen mentioned her forthcoming visit to China and addressed Margaret, wondering what her Chinese hosts might be wearing. That gave Margaret an opening to speak. She explained how in Houston the changing political and social climate in China had been reflected in the changing dress style of the Chinese Consul General and his wife at successive Consular receptions, from plain grey Mao suits for both of them in the first year through in the fourth year to black tie for the Consul-General and elaborately ornamented cocktail dress for his wife.

When people ask me about the 'kissing of hands' experience I tell them that Her Majesty is very well informed on every subject. She takes very seriously that the appointee is to be Her Ambassador representing the United Kingdom, not merely the representative of the government of the day. An Ambassador is after all the personal representative of one Head of State to another Head of State. The occasion was neither our first nor our last visit to Buckingham Palace, but the 'kissing of hands' was easily the most important and the most memorable.

I am especially pleased that I became one of Her Majesty's Ambassadors when such appointments warranted a personal meeting with The Queen. I have recently been told that twenty-five years after my appointment to Hanoi there are now so many appointments of Ambassadors, most of them to countries of little importance and of no great interest, that they are received at Buckingham Palace in batches of five at a time. In Gilbertian terms:

When every one is somebodee,
Then no one's anybody.

W. S. Gilbert was as 'right as right could be' in to-day's world, as he was when he wrote the *The Gondoliers*.

I saw appointment to Vietnam as an excellent opportunity to fill a gap in my experience of Asia as well as to assess whether I had been accurate in understanding the Vietnamese and their objectives at the time I was in Cambodia ten years earlier.

In 1985 the Vietnamese were still in occupation of much of Cambodia, having invaded in 1979 to eject the Khmer Rouge from Phnom Penh. To general international approval at the time the Vietnamese had turned the murderous Khmer Rouge out of Phnom Penh: only to find that having freed the Cambodian people from that particularly nasty regime, they had come under heavy criticism for remaining in occupation. Britain also joined others in condemning the continued incarceration in 're-education' camps of large numbers of southern Vietnamese; and we had our own problem in the influx of Vietnamese 'boat people' into Hong Kong. Those factors meant that as far as Vietnam was concerned Britain was the least friendly of all the Western countries that had diplomatic missions in Hanoi at the time. The French and Germans offered minor cultural exchanges: and the Australians had been helping with reforestation; but we British were not prepared to provide Vietnam with so much as a pianist to play in the Hanoi Opera House.

My first official duty was to call on the Foreign Minister to hand over the Letters of Recall of my predecessor and to deliver a copy of my letters of accreditation as Her Britannic Majesty's Ambassador Extraordinary and Plenipotentiary. Sadly the 'plenipotentiary' element of the title no longer has the significance that it had in previous centuries. I could only fantasise about getting up in the morning in a bad mood and declaring war before breakfast. The practice of a new Ambassador handing over the Letters of Recall of his predecessor was to emphasise the continuity of diplomatic relations by showing that there had not been, nor intended to be, any formal gap in representation at ambassadorial level. A new Ambassador's credentials would normally be later presented to the Head of State, though it was an indication of the coolness of formal relations between the United Kingdom and Vietnam that in the event I presented my credentials to the Vice-President, not to the Head of State himself.

When I made my first call on Nguyen Co Thach, the veteran Foreign Minister, he started our conversation with a smile as he said, 'I apologise that I learnt my English in India.' He was the only senior Vietnamese political figure I met who did speak fluent English; and he did do so with a slight touch of that attractive lilt that one hears with English when spoken by both Indians and the Welsh. I soon discovered however that quite a number of senior officials, especially those involved in trade in the south of the country and in the oil industry, spoke good English. It seemed that thirty years after the battle of Dien Bien Phu no Vietnamese under the age of forty spoke French.

Nguyen Co Thach gave the impression of being relaxed and friendly. Why shouldn't he? In his long time as Foreign Minister he had survived all his principal international opposition and had been on the winning side. Moving on to more formal business I said to him that I was sure he would understand that: '. . . as Prime Minister Margaret Thatcher said in the House of Commons on 27 July 1979, in the course of the debate on the economic summit in Tokyo of that year, and in answer to a question: "there will be no further assistance to Vietnam whilst present circumstances continue".' I then added, 'Those circumstances are: while Vietnam is in Cambodia; while Vietnam keeps the "re-education" camps open; and until we resolve the problem of the boat people arriving in Hong Kong. However,' I continued, 'there is nothing in my instructions that says that

Britain and Vietnam cannot do commercial business with each other. So until circumstances change I shall devote my time here as Ambassador to developing straightforward commercial relationships between Vietnamese organisations and British business.' I then bade the Foreign Minister good-bye and went back to the Embassy to get on with it.

The simplest description I can give of Vietnam in 1985 would be 'poor but honest'. It was certainly poor. We soon discovered it was also much poorer in Hanoi than in the south of the country and things weren't that good in the south either. There were no problems with garbage collection in the capital. Every possibly useful tin, paper or piece of plastic was removed from the residence at the end of each day when our servants went home. What little remained was left in the street to be picked over by the neighbours. By the time the municipal garbage collectors came past there was nothing left but a pile of small bits and pieces to be swept up.

When we told friends that we were going to Vietnam several were concerned that it might be dangerous. I was soon able to tell them that Hanoi was at the time probably the safest place on earth for a British Ambassador. There was no way any IRA terrorist would get past the tight immigration controls at the airport and the city had a highly developed system of 'neighbourhood watch'. In all our travels around Vietnam only once did our guide show concern for our security. We were driving from Saigon to the old French hill resort of Dalat and had delayed at a roadside shop. Our guide urged us to move on so that we would reach Dalat before dark as the pass through the hills ahead did have something of a reputation for occasional attacks by bandits.

Our first visit to Vung Tao in the south provided a sad but nonetheless interesting lesson in how the Vietnamese coped with those people who did not fit in and towards whom none of the traditional obligations applied. We were staying overnight at a hotel where it was clear that the food was not going to be very good. So we asked our guide if he could find a place for us to eat, bearing in mind that at that time there was not supposed to be any such thing as a private enterprise establishment of any kind. After some delay we were driven to a typical Chinese-style eating house open to the street. It was packed with local people.

We were enjoying a delicious meal when a group of eight arose from the table next to ours and left the restaurant. The departing diners had left all their plates on the table, most of them clearly having amounts of rice and other food still on them. There was no immediate attempt by the restaurant staff to clear the table. After a few moments a tiny child with hair that made it clear she was of mixed race and wearing a simple shabby dress, came in through the entrance of the restaurant bearing a large empty food tin. She went around the abandoned table and scraped into her tin all the rice and other food from every one of the plates left on the table. She then slipped out of the restaurant. No one in the restaurant, neither diners nor staff, took the slightest notice. The little girl was invisible. The diners would have felt no obligation to directly help a child who was obviously not a member of their community, but they would not interfere with her scavenging, something that was clearly of no surprise or concern to either them or to the people managing the restaurant.

Our first visit to Saigon provided lessons showing just how stupid the Communist system was. At the famous Rex Hotel the few foreigners in the city could, at a small store on the ground floor of the hotel, buy a can of warm Heineken beer for 50 US cents. We could then go to the roof terrace of the hotel and buy a well chilled Heineken beer in a nice glass served by an elderly waiter in a white coat and enjoy the drink while looking over the city as the sun set: price 50 US cents: surely the cheapest beer in Asia.

Our room at the Rex was very run-down. The plumbing didn't work properly and the air-conditioner rattled away all night to no great effect. The price of the room was $50 US a night. I talked to the manager of the hotel pointing out that the Rex was the only hotel at which foreigners would want to stay and would quite happily pay $200 a night or more. Why didn't the hotel put up the prices and spend the extra money on doing up the hotel rooms? The manager sadly replied, 'It doesn't work like that. Whatever extra money the hotel receives goes to the local People's Committee.' So why bother? It has all changed since then. There are many first class hotels, the Rex has been renovated and added to, and the beer costs much more than 50 US cents a glass. What hasn't changed is the roof terrace at the Rex and Margaret and I return to the hotel whenever we revisit Saigon.

Developing commercial trade was going to be a slow and difficult business, but as time went by I was able to give some useful advice to some British companies. Unlike my time in South Korea however I could not expect to see any results appear in the trade figures for Vietnam while I was still in post. The low status of Vietnam in British political thinking of the time meant that I would be trying to develop trade when there were no offers of credit, no special aid, nothing that is usually available to oil the wheels of commerce in developing a new market. I gradually came to realise however that, as had been the case in South Korea, some British goods were appearing in Vietnam, doing so as re-exports from Singapore and Hong Kong rather than being sold directly from the UK. There were also one or two British companies that had significant exports to Vietnam but were doing so from manufacturing subsidiaries in Singapore

Castrol Oil was already, by 1985, doing one or two million dollars worth of business out of Singapore, but any British interest in that trade, direct or indirect, did not appear as British exports. The lubricating oil did however represent Singapore trade with Vietnam at a time when Singapore was one of the countries urging Britain not to trade with that country. Spare parts and other industrial bits and pieces turned up through Singapore. BAT's State Express 555 cigarettes were in effect the third currency in Vietnam at the time, but the Singapore factory that produced them didn't even realise they were entering Vietnam in any significant quantity. When I met with BAT's subsidiary company during a visit to Singapore it was clear that they had no idea of the status value that their brand held in Vietnam. Scotch whisky was of course always to be found in Hanoi if needed, while Coca Cola and Pepsi were later widespread throughout Vietnam long before the United States opened up direct trade relations with Vietnam.

Most of the trade that did go on with the 'West' at that time was through indirect channels involving Chinese traders in Hong Kong and Singapore, traders who could use a variety of informal and indirect channels of their own, employing in many cases their traditional contacts with the remaining Chinese community.

So there was not a great deal I or my staff could do for trade promotion, especially compared with the Japanese who had a number of long-term company 'resident' representatives and who at the time of my first visit to Saigon were holding their second post-1980 industrial trade exhibition under the sponsorship of the Vietnam-Japan Trade Association. Foreigners were not supposed to see the exhibition but I was already beginning to develop a good relationship with the Vietnamese and my 'guide' from Saigon Tourist took me to the out-of-the-way suburban location for the exhibition. I was welcomed warmly by the Japanese representatives, who happily showed me around their show. As one would expect, it was clear that the Japanese exhibits were very cleverly targeted at those sectors where early growth could be expected as economic conditions improved. There was even a saloon motor-car on display – just to whet the local appetite.

Strictly speaking there were no foreign residents in Vietnam at that time – other than diplomats. So if a British company had suggested placing a representative in Vietnam the official answer would be 'not possible'. But orientals are clever people, especially when it comes to business. One day a pleasant Japanese businessman called on me bearing a file of telex messages. He explained that his Japanese principals had told him that a British company with which they had a relationship had heard from me about possible opportunities in Vietnam. Could he be of any help? Over a cup of coffee I asked him how long he had been in Vietnam. 'Three years,' he replied. But 'How can you do that when no foreigners are allowed visas to be resident in Vietnam?' I asked. He explained that he entered on a routinely permitted three month visa and at the end of each three months he went to Bangkok for a few days and obtained a fresh visa for another three months. No major Japanese companies were however at that time present in Vietnam under their own names. The trade was carried on under the names of small discreet 'sister companies'. This meant that if the great Japanese companies were asked internationally whether they were doing business with Vietnam, or had representatives in the country, they could answer more or less truthfully, 'No.'

It soon became apparent to me that there was very little business that could be done by British firms on a direct commercial basis. The Vietnamese official trading companies certainly appeared to have little money available for use at their own discretion. An exception was the Saigon Trading Company, the trading arm of the Saigon provincial government. It was the Bulgarian Ambassador who later gave me a clue as to how the provincial trading companies, as compared to the central government bodies, were actually able to do significant import and export business on their own. The Bulgarian bemoaned the fact that he was supposed to obtain some repayment of past Bulgarian assistance to Vietnam by negotiating shipments of rubber and other products from the central government trading companies. 'But the central government trading companies have no rubber, coffee or other products; and I do not have the staff to send round the country to negotiate with the provincial trading companies that do have such commodities to export.' The provincial trading companies were much happier exporting to Hong Kong and Singapore in exchange for US dollars than supplying countries such as Bulgaria.

I was able to develop a good relationship with the Vietnamese oil industry by helping them out with a problem they had with obtaining delivery from Singapore of some urgently needed lubricating material. A Soviet oil-drilling ship was in Singapore for maintenance and was about to leave to return to Vietnamese waters. The Vietnamese had ordered some special lubricating material from Shell in Singapore but were having difficulty in getting the necessary confirmed letters of credit in time for the suppliers to agree to deliver the material to the Soviet ship before the latter sailed.

I decided that, knowing PetroViet really did have priority access to foreign exchange, and that the total amount involved would not bankrupt me if something went wrong. I would immediately send telex messages from the Rex Hotel to both the supplying companies, strongly recommending that the lubricants ordered be delivered to the Soviet ship. The Petro Viet officials offered to let me use their telex. Why not? Their telex was probably a lot more reliable than that at the Rex Hotel and the Vietnamese would in any event read whatever I sent in a telex message sent from the hotel. In my telex I explained who I was and said that the material was urgently needed; and if it was not shipped aboard the Soviet vessel there would be significant delay while the Vietnamese found some other way to have the goods shipped to Vung Tao, the headquarters for the offshore oil activity. I assured Shell that the explanation for the Vietnamese difficulty in getting the necessary financial documentation completed was genuine and that I was personally quite sure of their good faith.

The goods were shipped; the suppliers received payment; and I developed significant credit with the Vietnamese oil industry, credit that undoubtedly helped when the time came to introduce British companies to that industry. This case was also another illustration that while telling the British government that Britain should not trade with Vietnam, Singapore was certainly not going to do anything to hinder its own business with the same country.

Most helpful to us personally was that, unlike all other foreign embassies, we were not required to change our domestic staff each year. Colleagues would complain that every year they had to take on and train a new set of servants. We on the other hand had a housekeeper and a houseman, both of whom had been with the Embassy residence for as long as anyone could remember. I discovered at the end of our stay in Hanoi that one reason our domestic staffing arrangements were left undisturbed year after year may have been that Madame Hong our housekeeper was the sister of a Vice-Minister. I only discovered that family connection of Madame Hong when at the last Queen's Birthday Party we hosted she thanked me for inviting her brother to the reception.

The houseman, Dong, had been with the residence for many years. He wasn't very efficient but he was willing and friendly. He would occasionally sit on the floor at Margaret's feet in the study and chat with her. He told her that he had been at Dien Bien Phu – but 'on the wrong side'. It may well have been his experiences there and afterwards that left him with what we felt was a slightly off-beat personality. I am sure that the staff, who did not live on the premises but went home each evening, were regularly grilled by the Vietnamese security as to what went on in the residence. Margaret and I spent many years living on the assumption that we were being listened to one way or another, so it didn't worry us. But whatever, we became very fond of the staff we had and tried not to rub in to our Western colleagues that we did not have the problems they experienced with repeated changes of domestic servants.

We looked after our staff well. When they worked overtime to assist with an evening function at the residence we were expected to pay them overtime. If we did so through official channels it would be calculated in local currency. By the time they might receive payment it would be of little value. We could not give them US$ as it would have been an offence on our part to do so and an offence on their part to be in possession of foreign currency. But we could pay them in the third currency, State Express 555 cigarettes – no other brand would do. The cigarettes were not for smoking but to trade in the market at the equivalent of 1US$ or 15,000 dong for each pack. With two packets of 555s the staff went home smiling.

The Embassy Residence in Hanoi was a most unusual building. The house had started its life as a purpose-built French up-market brothel, located close to the Opera House and the 'Raffles' of Hanoi: the Hotel Metropole. It was of solid construction but of a modest size compared to all other Ambassadors' residences in Hanoi. In addition to the kitchens and laundry area the house had been designed with six bedrooms, four upstairs and two downstairs, each *en suite* with a traditional Asian bathroom; two sitting-rooms and three entrances, with a generous hall downstairs and landing upstairs. The design offered endless potential for classic French bedroom farce. All the principal rooms were octagonal in shape, apparently a traditionally 'happy' design. Some adjustment had been made to the layout when adapted to ambassadorial use, though the only significant structural change was to enable one of the downstairs sitting-rooms to be extended to provide a dining-room that could seat fourteen. Of the downstairs bedrooms one had been adapted to provide a second sitting-room and one into a utility room. Of the four original bedrooms two were furnished as bedrooms each with its small but modernised bathroom. A third upstairs bedroom provided a study and the fourth a small private sitting-room.

Number 15 Phan Chu Trinh was a pleasant home for us and was very convenient to the building that at the time housed the Embassy Chancery. We were tempted to believe that through all the troubles Hanoi had experienced any ghosts in our temporary home would have been contented ones. A not so happy legend about the residence had it that the son of the French General Jean Lattre de Tassigny spent his last night in the house before being killed by the Viet Minh. Margaret and I did sometimes feel rather guilty that while the two of us had eight rooms at our disposal the somewhat larger but very run-down traditional French villa next door housed Vietnamese families numbering about sixty people in all. We felt even more guilt when occasional power cuts led us to start up the large generator that Her Majesty's Government had provided and placed in what had at some stage been a garage. Instead of a small and adequate Japanese-made generator London had provided a large high-revving machine that was also extremely noisy and made life intolerable for the Vietnamese in the crowded villa next door – especially the old man trying to sleep in the space next to our garage wall.

I found Vietnamese food rather bland, having developed a taste for the spicier food of Singapore and South Korea. But one item I remember well was the huge freshwater snails that were occasionally offered. They bore no resemblance to *escargots* raw or cooked, except that they came in the same shape of shell. I discovered later that these monster snails were farmed in the lakes around Hanoi. They were the *pièce de résistance* of the simple farewell dinner given to me at the end of my time in Hanoi. When I later discovered that the lakes were also the repositories of sundry wastewater from the city I realised that it might have been reckless to eat the snails. Nonetheless I would certainly try them again; but on later visits have been unable to find them on any menu or even to meet a tourist who has been offered them.

It was particularly interesting for me to be in direct contact for the first time with Soviet and East European diplomats. I sometimes say that all my humorous stories from Vietnam came from the East Germans and the Bulgarians. I have mentioned earlier the Bulgarians' problem of obtaining commodities in repayment for all the assistance Bulgaria had given North Vietnam during the war.

The East German Ambassador told me his tale of their first major aid project to Vietnam after 1975. He said that the East German government had offered to build in Vietnam a complete textile mill with the intention of providing a mill with established proven technology. But the Vietnamese, having – as the Ambassador said – just won a war, were confident that they could do anything and insisted that East Germany provide a textile mill equipped with nothing less than the latest high technology. So the Germans agreed and asked the Vietnamese to nominate the site for the mill. The site turned out to be in a location with difficult access for transport of raw material in and finished product out. There was also an inadequate water supply and whenever there was a shortage of water priority of supply went to the nearby rice fields. The plant was however built and there was a grand hand-over ceremony at which the Germans offered to leave a technical team at the mill to help the locals get it working. The East German Ambassador put the Vietnamese answer as being nothing less than 'No. No. Get out. We will manage it.' Three months later the Vietnamese came to the East Germans and said, 'Your mill doesn't work!'

The East Germans had had quite a long business arrangement with the Vietnamese involving the manufacture of men's suits. The East German Ambassador explained to me that they would ship to Vietnam a quantity of material sufficient to make a hundred suits, but they started getting back not a hundred suits but more like ninety-seven. When they tackled their Vietnamese partners in the business it was explained to the Germans that the factory had to have the 'missing suits' to sell, as that was the only means the factory had of obtaining any funds that they could control and use for minor maintenance and so on. My German colleague told me that the problem had been solved by shipping from East Germany enough material for 103 suits but doing so in the expectation of receiving only a hundred in return.

Calling on the Soviet Ambassador was most interesting. It was at the time that Gorbachev was exhorting Russians to work harder and for officials to eat less caviar and drink less vodka. Happily at the time when I made my courtesy call on my Soviet colleague Gorbachov's message had not got through to the Soviet Embassy in Hanoi. Nonetheless it was just as well that at eleven o'clock in the morning there was not much temptation to consume more than a ceremonial two shots of vodka. The caviar was excellent and plentiful.

Before being posted to Hanoi, Boris Tchaplin, the Soviet Ambassador, had been a very senior official in charge of some eastern part of the Soviet Union. After Hanoi he became a Vice-Minister in the Foreign Ministry in Moscow. So he was undoubtedly someone worth getting to know and to talk to – even though talking to him meant through an interpreter. My view was that whatever an 'Eastern' colleague said about Vietnam I always double and triple checked elsewhere before assuming the information I was given was reliable. But a colleague's comments were always a good starting point and one could soon assess whether what he said was good value.

The most extraordinary thing I found out about Boris Tchaplin was that although he had been in Hanoi for thirteen years not one of the Western Ambassadors, including my predecessors, had ever thought to invite him to dinner. When I told Margaret of this situation she immediately saw it as a challenge. At the next meeting of diplomatic wives she met the Soviet Ambassador's wife and promptly asked, through the wife's interpreter, whether she and her husband would come to have dinner with us. The immediate response was positive. The event turned out to be the most worthwhile 'diplomatic' dinner we ever gave anywhere.

The attitude of my colleagues and my staff was that 'he wouldn't accept an invitation'. Rubbish. Of course he would not accept an invitation extended to him alone. An invitation had to be extended in terms of: 'Would you and your wife come to dinner with us and would you like to bring one or two of your colleagues with you?' That immediately allowed the guest to bring a 'minder' with him when he went to dine with 'the enemy'. In the event Boris Tchaplin not only brought his No 2 as the 'minder' but also brought two excellent interpreters. For my part, as Britain was at the time also 'representing' the EU, I did the decent thing and invited my German, French and Italian colleagues and their wives. Boris Tchaplin's wife was a delightful table companion, even though she spoke no English. Her interpreter was excellent. Margaret had a similar experience with the Ambassador and his interpreter at the other end of the dining table. The after-dinner conversations with the two principal Soviet guests went on until well after midnight. My European colleagues then wondered why they hadn't thought of doing the same and they kindly included us in the guest list for subsequent dinner parties when they invited the Tchaplins.

I found a similar discouraging attitude to my proposals for inviting Vietnamese officials to lunch at the residence. 'They won't come.' Rubbish. Of course they would love to come but you could not just ask an official by himself. The formula was, as with the Soviets: 'Would you come to lunch and bring one or two of your colleagues with you?' It worked every time. If one of my own staff had gone off to an East European embassy on his own he might have been on the next plane back to London. My rule was that only I could make such calls unaccompanied.

The Chinese and French Embassies were always worth being invited to. The French undoubtedly still had something of a special relationship with Vietnamese people if not with their government. If one wanted to know what was happening in the politics of Hanoi that day, it was the French who would be most likely to know. On the other hand the Chinese always seemed to know much more than anybody else about what was going on in the longer term.

The Chinese Ambassador was in a rather difficult situation. He was allowed to travel outside Hanoi only when the Vietnamese arranged an annual outing for the whole Diplomatic Corps – on such occasions they could hardly exclude him. Although an unusual situation it is not unknown when relations between two countries are at a difficult state. The practice towards the Chinese in Hanoi did suggest that similar restrictions were being imposed on the Vietnamese Ambassador in Beijing. Another tit-for-tat restriction can be on the number of personnel at an Embassy who are granted full diplomatic status.

When giving talks about Vietnam I always point out that Vietnamese history amounts to two thousand years of determination to be independent of China: one thousand years fighting for independence and one thousand years fighting to remain independent. That is of course a simplification; but it is a version that resonates with Vietnamese who have told me on more than one occasion that the issue that dominates all Vietnamese thinking is the relationship with China.

Another matter that is often not remembered is that it was not the Chinese who were the main supporters of the Vietnamese in the fighting against the Americans. The main supporters were the Soviets. When I was in Cambodia there were stories that China was being obstructive to Soviet wishes to supply North Vietnam by sending military supplies through China by rail. That situation is borne out by the fact that there were often several Soviet cargo ships in the northern port of Hai Phong during the war. It was of considerable embarrassment to Washington when a careless bombing incident damaged a Soviet ship.

My own view is that China would not have minded in the least if North Vietnam had failed in its attempt to unify the country, nor how much of the north's infrastructure was destroyed by the Americans. Both circumstances would have resulted in a very weak North Vietnam as neighbour to China. On the other hand I have long maintained that North Vietnam could never compromise about unification with the South. North Vietnam is an economic deficiency region dependent on the importation of as much as three million tonnes of rice each year, ideally from the 'rice bowl' of the Mekong delta in the South. Without unification of North and South Vietnam the North would have been at the mercy of China, dependent on whatever help it could continue to receive from the Soviet bloc.

When Margaret and I drove into Hai Phong on our first visit we passed a large building of the traditional French style and I asked the driver what it was. He said it was the headquarters of Hai Phong People's Committee, in other words of the city's government. So we stopped and I walked in to pay a courtesy visit. I was warmly welcomed and asked if we could return in an hour or so as they would like us to be their guests at lunch. After stocking-up with fresh prawns at the fish market, filling the Embassy stock of *eskis*, we returned to the headquarters building. We were treated to a delightful lunch with the local Secretary of the Communist Party as our host. During the lunch I commented on the fact that the building clearly dated from the French period. Our host said that while the centre of Hai Phong had been untouched he and his seven-year-old daughter had stood on the balcony outside the room in which we were lunching and watched the suburbs being carpet-bombed. Our host later moved to a senior position in the Party in Hanoi and turned up as an official guest at our last Queen's Birthday Party where he greeted us as old friends.

The United States Air Force flattened everything in North Vietnam except the port of Hai Phong and the centre of Hanoi. The former was left alone because of the risk of doing serious damage to Soviet ships bringing in supplies, or even to the small British-flag Hong Kong registered ships visiting the port.

The centre of Hanoi was left alone by the American bombing because there were living in the city quite a few Western diplomats, including a British Consul-General and the Canadian representative of the International Commission that had been set up after the French defeat in 1954 to try and get settlement between North and South Vietnam. The Canadian Commissioner was killed by a stray American bomb. The British Consul-General, Dame Daphne Park, many years later said publicly that she had spent some of her time in Hanoi 'bomb-spotting' for the Americans. No doubt she did all the bomb-spotting she could from riding about Hanoi on her bicycle but I doubt whether she was given the opportunity to see what was going on further afield.

Few people seem to recall that in 1979, when the Vietnamese entered Cambodia, China invaded North Vietnam and did so sending an estimated 200,000 troops through the traditional invasion route of the Lang Son Pass. To the Chinese surprise their army got a 'bloody nose' and withdrew, but not before the population of Hanoi had been warned to evacuate the capital at twenty-four hours notice. I suspect that one factor in 1979 was that the Chinese PLA had not done any serious fighting since the Korean War, whereas the Vietnamese were not only defending their home territory but their soldiers had just concluded twenty years of serious front-line battling.

A Chinese military offensive of a rather different type came about while we were in Hanoi. It caused a lot of excitement in London and elsewhere, including with one of my staff who was on his first Asian post and didn't perhaps understand what he was seeing and hearing. What happened was that, at a time when Singapore and Thailand were demanding that the Vietnamese leave Cambodia, China made an announcement that they had fired 50,000 rounds of artillery into northern Vietnam. The Chinese declared that their action was to punish the Vietnamese for staying in occupation of their neighbour. Many thought the artillery barrage was a prelude to another Chinese invasion. My first query was: 'Where did all this artillery barrage take place?' When the answer was that the event was near the border in the far north-west of Vietnam I immediately realised that there was nothing to be alarmed about. The Chinese knew that the Vietnamese knew that no one was going to start a war there. If the artillery fire had been at the Lang Son Pass area north of Hanoi, then that would have been a different matter altogether.

It was almost a classic instance of the Chinese dragon huffing and puffing to put on a show for the benefit of Western governments, governments that would be pleased to see that China was taking a serious view of the Vietnamese presence in Cambodia. To prove my assumption I went to our in-house Vietnamese 'fixer' and asked him to obtain a permit for me to drive up to the Chinese border at Lang Son. He looked surprised but did what I asked and the permit arrived. I set off in the Embassy Land-Rover with just the driver. We went without interruption all the way to the border town of Lang Son – a town destroyed completely in the 1979 Chinese attack.

After visiting the town we set off to return to the capital. After a mile or so the driver stopped and pointed to a narrow dirt road leading off through the hills to the north. 'That is the road to the Chinese border; do you want to go there?' Being good at knowing if not perhaps always observing the rules, I asked whether my travel permit covered that area. 'No,' the driver replied, 'but if you want to we can go there.' So we turned off the main road and proceeded along the narrow unmade dirt track. We passed through two military check points where the bored-looking guards simply raised the barrier as we approached and showed no interest in the flag-bearing diplomatic vehicle passing their way. Eventually the driver began to show some signs of nervousness. He stopped the vehicle. Pointing to the hills immediately ahead he said, 'Chinese rockets up there,' clearly suggesting he thought it was time we turned round.

When we got back to Hanoi I attended an evening diplomatic reception and asked a Vietnamese minister: 'What are you doing about all this Chinese artillery fire?' The minister smiled, replying, 'We respond in proportion to our population.'

My jaunt to the frontier gave me material for a useful note to the Defence Attaché at the Embassy at Bangkok. In relating the story of my drive to the frontier I mentioned that on the way we passed a number of Vietnamese military posts at none of which were there any signs of active military preparedness. We also passed, quite a long way north of Hanoi, an area where the road and railway ran close together and where a large number of army road fuel-tankers had gathered. The soldiers at the site were all clearly relaxed, sitting in the sun or playing football. It didn't take much observation to realise that the fuel trucks had gathered together from military positions along the defended frontier region to wait for a train to arrive that night carrying fuel with which to replenish, under cover of darkness, the fuel supplies for military units along the frontier. The proximity of rail to road made it easy to identify the location on any map of the area.

My note to the Defence Attaché might have been of some professional interest to him but was of no real significance to British interests. It could however have been an example of why the Vietnamese did not want Chinese diplomats wandering about the countryside.

Just as there was a misinterpretation in London of the Chinese intentions over the firing of 50,000 artillery shells into Vietnam, so there was another error over interpreting the entries in the official Hanoi diplomatic list. The Foreign Office prepared a memorandum for some purpose or other that included the statement that 'China maintains a residual diplomatic presence in Hanoi'. This might be said to be correct if measured by the number of Chinese officials given diplomatic status in Hanoi, but was wildly incorrect if considering the size of the Chinese Embassy.

What had happened was that someone in my office had sent off to London a copy of the Hanoi Diplomatic List which did indeed show only six names against the entry for the Chinese Embassy; even the British Embassy had more names on the List than the Chinese. I found it necessary to write and advise London that there were a hundred or more diplomats and officials, commercial attachés, defence attachés, and so on, working within the Chinese Embassy. The point was that the Vietnamese would only grant diplomatic status to six of them. This again may have been a tit-for-tat for China's treatment of the Vietnamese diplomatic staff in Beijing.

The Chinese diplomats may not have been permitted to travel outside Hanoi but they could be counted upon to have read everything printed within Vietnam. Dinners at the Chinese Embassy were not only most agreeable but also very interesting for their interpretation of what was going on around the country, an interpretation based on what the Vietnamese were telling their own people in print or on the radio.

One of Napoleon's *obiter dicta* about diplomats and diplomacy was: 'An Ambassador is after all nothing more than a titled spy.' I might agree; but

Napoleon's remark does not mean that an Ambassador needs to seek information surreptitiously or rely on whispered comments made in the shadows down dark alleys by people who can't be trusted by anyone. An Ambassador who understands his host country, and who also has wide experience and knowledge and knows what to look for, can learn a great deal from just keeping his eyes, ears and mind open while travelling about, without doing anything to which the host country could take exception. They can always confine diplomats to the capital city if they wish to do so.

I was able to report evidence that Singapore and Thailand were trading with Vietnam while those countries were at the same time telling the UK and others not to do business there. My maritime background meant I easily recognised Bangkok registered ships alongside the wharves in Saigon; and my straightforward commercial contact with the Vietnamese oil industry revealed that they were having no 'sanction' type difficulties in buying lubricants in Singapore. Even my enthusiasm for anything to do with railways led me to be curious about the railroad route north of Hanoi towards the border, while my brief period of working with an oil company made me particularly curious about the gathering of 500-gallon fuel trucks.

The railway from Hanoi to Lang Son had been built as standard gauge with Chinese assistance after World War 2. Much of it was destroyed in 1979 and has not been rebuilt, perhaps because the rail connection was recognised after the 1979 invasion as a weakness in defence of the frontier so close to Hanoi. On the other hand the longer route to the border in the north-west has been modernised. But that railway is metre gauge and does not therefore provide a continuous rail connection with the Chinese railways. Together with its terminus on the remote border, that railway does not provide the same possible facility to assist any invasion force. Such matters may in any event now have much less significance in an age of warfare by rockets and other modern weapons.

It is perhaps an irony that the Vietnamese incursion into Cambodia became something of 'Vietnam's own Vietnam' in domestic political terms. As the Vietnamese army stayed on in Cambodia there were increasing numbers of injured Vietnamese soldiers being repatriated. It became impossible to prevent news of such casualties spreading about the country. The World Health Organisation representative told me that there was also increasing evidence of malaria being brought back from Cambodia, with the worrying aspect that neglect within Cambodia meant that it appeared new drug-resistant strains of the disease were appearing.

The third factor that came to notice of the Vietnamese population in the South was that while the officers in the army all tended to come from the North, the private soldiers who bore most of the casualties were almost all conscripted from the South. The issues were beginning to become a serious domestic problem. By 1987 it was becoming clearly in Vietnam's own interest to get out of Cambodia as soon as possible.

In 1985 and for some years afterwards there was no official American presence in Vietnam. So I twice entertained American congressional delegations to breakfast to enable them to get a briefing from myself and my European Community colleagues. They were visiting Hanoi to talk with the Vietnamese especially about the issue of Missing In Action servicemen still unaccounted for. I was very impressed with the Senate Foreign Relations Committee visitors. We talked about the MIA issue and current developments generally. I remember the Chairman of the Senate team pointing out that after World War 2 and the Korean War the number of MIAs unaccounted for never got below 20 per cent but that by 1985 the number unaccounted for in Vietnam was down to four and a half per cent.

The French Ambassador told the group that he was certain the Vietnamese were being truthful when they said that there were no live Americans under the control of the Vietnamese authorities. He said that it could not be ruled out that a few Americans might have been left behind and living hidden in the local economy. He related how only a few weeks earlier an elderly Frenchman had turned up at the French Embassy. The French soldier had gone AWOL and stayed behind when the French army went home. He had lived in Hai Phong since 1954 with a Vietnamese wife. His wife had died and the old French soldier was ill and homesick for France. He came to the Embassy asking to be sent home. Many Americans of Hispanic or mixed backgrounds could fit in quite well in Vietnam as far as appearance is concerned.

The breakfasts themselves were much appreciated by the American delegations. Hotel catering was very poor indeed at that time, even at the Vietnamese official guest-houses at which foreign official visitors were accommodated. There was no such thing as an independent restaurant. Not long after the Senate Foreign Relations Committee visit, a mixed Congressional Foreign Relations Committee group arrived. In the mixed Senate and House of Representatives group I regret to say that some of the Congressmen were not all that impressive. Those who came to breakfast told me quite seriously that one of their number hadn't joined the breakfast because – as it was put to us – 'He wanted to walk round the "Hanoi Hilton" in case he would hear an American voice from inside the prison singing "God Bless America".' Some people just don't want to have their political illusions spoilt by reality.

I have for many years since my first enlightening casual encounter with a Soviet diplomat in Jakarta in 1966, questioned the extent to which the Vietnamese and the Chinese governments were true Marxists. I find it hard to believe that peoples so deeply imbued with centuries of Confucianism and by nationalism would for long defer to an ideology thought up by a johnny-come-lately German and adopted by Russians. But in the period following the first World War China was in chaos and Vietnam was making no progress towards independence from France, so who would help them?

Ho Chi Minh was a young fervent nationalist when he was in Europe at the time of the Versailles Peace Conference. His attempts to obtain support for an independent Vietnam made no progress whatever, which is understandable if one now reads what a mess that conference was. The only people who would listen to Ho Chi Minh and offer support were the Bolsheviks. The Bolsheviks were quite happy to support any group likely to further their aim of world-wide revolution. For his part, Ho Chi Minh was quite happy to genuflect before images of Marx if that was the only way to get support for Vietnamese independence. So he was quite prepared to return to Asia and set up a Vietnamese Communist Party. After the second World War Ho Chi Minh and his fellow nationalists thought there was a second chance for independence from France but that hope was also frustrated in the repeat of Western concern about the stability of France and the threat of Communism in Europe. I have a facsimile copy of a letter written by Ho Chi Minh in 1945 that makes interesting reading, just as the origins of the letter are themselves worth noting.

On numerous occasions, I have, on cruise ships, given a talk about Vietnam. I always make it clear that I am interested in talking about Vietnam's history up until the battle of Dien Bien Phu in 1954 and developments after 1975. I do not talk about what the Vietnamese always refer to as 'The American War'. On one occasion an elderly American came up to me from the audience and said, 'I was at Dien Bien Phu in

1945.' I did not think anyone had heard of that place until it became famous in history as the site of the defeat of the French in 1954. The passenger, Mr Ned Carpenter, lent me a copy of a small book, *MisX*, written by Colonel A. R. Wichtrich. The Colonel had commanded a secret unit, AGAS, responsible for recovering US pilots downed over China and Vietnam in 1944–45. Ned Carpenter had himself flown into Dien Bien Phu in 1945 to pick up a small group of American pilots.

In *MisX* Colonel Wichtrich records how he received help from the Vietnamese, who were hoping to obtain independence for Vietnam at the end of the war and to do so in accordance with the principles of the Atlantic Charter, signed by Roosevelt and Churchill and defining the rights of all peoples to 'self-determination and to self-government'.

The Colonel was intrigued by the ability of the Vietnamese to build a secret airfield in the jungle and the existence even in 1945 of a jungle route known as the 'Ho Chi Minh trail'.

He records how helpful the Vietnamese nationalist movement was in the task of locating and recovering downed American pilots. The leader of the Vietnamese wrote a letter to Colonel Wichtrich. Part of the letter reads:

> In the general rejoicing of the victory of the Allies, victory of democracy and freedom over fascism & oppression – we feel a bit sorry, 1) our American friends are leaving us, 2) we have none or very small share in that democracy & freedom.
>
> Anyhow, we will keep on fighting to get our full share. In our first, we remain sure that the sympathy of the great people of America is with us. And when we attain our aim – National independence, We are sure to meet our American friends again . . . in happier conditions and in larger number.

The letter was signed in Western style: 'C. M. Ho' – i.e. Ho Chi Minh.

The result of the Vietnamese disappointment at being ignored in 1945, as they were in 1919, in their efforts to obtain independence from France led inevitably – as Ho Chi Minh predicted in 1945 – to the subsequent wars that went on until 1975.

The Soviets supported Ho Chi Minh and the Vietnamese nationalist movement right through from 1919 to 1975 and for a little while longer. But in 1986 it was the Soviet ambassador who told me that 'We have told the Vietnamese that we cannot afford to go on supporting them.' A hint perhaps that might have given advance notice to the West that the Soviet system was beginning to show signs of general collapse. It now seems clear that the Vietnamese had begun to realise that they should perhaps change their allegiance from Marxism to modified capitalism.

The change away from a system dominated by deference to Soviet attitudes began quite slowly. The first key decision was made at the Communist Party of Vietnam Congress in 1986. Always bright at dialectics the Vietnamese were certainly quite clever in justifying their damascene conversion from being declared Marxists to being in favour of the open market. At the 1986 Congress, when they made the first declaration of an intention to move towards a market economy, the Vietnamese 'Communists' managed to support the change by a quotation from Lenin: ' We must remember what Lenin said about the desire of ordinary people to own private property.' This was rather like reading into the Bible whatever suits you best. In this case, if Lenin said it, it must be all right! Lenin himself planned a similar U-turn in 1921 when he introduced the New Economic Policies to modify the Marxist policies that were ruining the new Soviet Union. The NEPs were then themselves reversed by Stalin.

From observations on my subsequent visits it appears that the Vietnamese wasted little time in taking down the pictures of Lenin and Marx. Pictures of the trio, Ho Chi Minh, Lenin and Marx were on every official wall when I was living in Vietnam. For years from 1990 onwards I safely defied anyone to find a picture of Lenin or Marx on an office wall anywhere in Vietnam today. But like most Asians, the Vietnamese are pragmatic. It cost me $20 for a donation to charity when, in Vung Tao in 1999, it was pointed out to me that there were portraits of Lenin and Marx on one particular street. The location of the portraits happened to be right opposite the headquarters of the still-operating Russian-Vietnam joint oil exploration and production company. The statue of Lenin in Hanoi survives but that was only erected in 1985 and his place in Vietnam's history might well justify it remaining in much the same way that the regicide Oliver Cromwell still has a statue in London.

The changes since 1987 have been truly remarkable. My wife and I have been back to Vietnam many times since 1987. It is a new world for ordinary Vietnamese. Vietnam and its people may still have a long way to go but, to paraphrase Harold Macmillan's words: 'The Vietnamese have never had it so good, ever.' Hanoi, which was unbelievably dull in our time there, with really nowhere decent for a foreigner to eat outside an embassy, has now got numerous excellent hotels and a whole range of restaurants. The superbly restored Metropole Hotel in Hanoi was a mouldering rat-infested pile in our day. The representative of the International Red Cross and his wife lived for years in a two-room suite, cooking on an improvised stove in their bathroom, yet still managing to entertain us to dinner. The country has changed dramatically, not just in Hanoi but in the provincial towns and villages. When considering the attitude that the Vietnamese people now have towards the outside world it is worth noting that more than half of today's population were not even born when the fighting ended in 1975.

In 1987 I came to the end of my two-year posting to Vietnam. One could see the potential for business in the country, but it was really too early to have achieved anything really exciting in commercial terms. Certainly for a commercial diplomat there was little one could really get started and hope to see any results while still in post. Margaret and I would not wish to have missed the experience. It is a beautiful country.

A final formality was my farewell call on the Foreign Minister. I made a point of saying exactly what I had said two years earlier. That is, I repeated word for word what I had said on my first call on him in 1985. 'As Prime Minister Mrs Margaret Thatcher said in the course of a debate in the House of Commons on 27 July 1979 " . . . there would be no further assistance to Vietnam while present circumstances continue; that is while Vietnam is in Cambodia, while the re-education camps continue, and until we settle the problem of the boat people arriving in Hong Kong".' Nguyen Co Thach smiled and said, 'We would like you to know that we respect the consistency of British policy.' He then added, 'And what is more, we agree with it. We have to get out of Cambodia, we must close the re-education camps and we must settle the boat people problem.' That seems to me to be almost the perfect note on which to end my diplomatic career.

Postscript

I AM FROM TIME TO TIME ASKED how I came to represent both Australia and the United Kingdom. I like to say that it just shows what a good diplomat I was that two countries were prepared to trust me with at least of few of their Top Secrets.

In reality it probably would not be so easy to arrange to-day. I am however old enough to have grown up in days of Empire. My first passport described me as 'British Subject: Citizen of the United Kingdom and Colonies'. The magic words were 'British Subject'. I was commissioned in the Royal Australian Naval Reserve in 1953 – with my commission signed by Field Marshal William Slim in his capacity as Governor General of Australia; by 1962 I had been elected to the Hobart City Council; I had stood as a candidate for the Tasmanian House of Assembly – obviously unsuccessfully; I had every intention of standing for Federal Parliament in due course – a quirk of fate shut that idea out of possibility. For none of those was it necessary to be an Australian citizen. At the time all that mattered was to be a British Subject. To borrow the motto of The Most Distinguished Order of Saint Michael and Saint George: *Auspicium Melioris Aevi*: 'token of a better age', perhaps?

The letter advising me of my appointment as an Australian Trade Commissioner included some wording that came as a surprise: 'While it is not essential, we think it would be helpful if when representing Australia you travelled on an Australian diplomatic passport; would you mind becoming an Australian citizen?' Of course not. As a member of the Royal Australian Naval Reserve I was prepared to risk my life defending Australia, I had stood for Parliament, and had ideas of becoming Prime Minister of Australia; it just hadn't occurred to me to become an Australian citizen. How agreeable to become an Australian by invitation. And I kept up my commitment to membership of the Reserve for a total of thirty-eight years until they retired me on grounds of old age.

My career as a British diplomat was certainly unusual. Through a series of five overseas postings I was never anything other than either 'Head of Post' or what is, in today's Americanised diplomacy, 'Deputy Head of

Mission'. And the good thing about being No 2 is that one always spends a considerable amount of time acting as No 1.

I soon came to realise that it was much more fun, and likely to produce more interesting experiences, if one was at the head of a smaller post rather than being No 5 or No 6 in a large Embassy in a city such as Paris or Tokyo. If the 'small post' was classified also as a 'hardship' post, so much the better. My career resulted in rather more than my share of promotions and decorations for such a short time in Her Majesty's Diplomatic Service, a career that began when I was ten years older than the usual age for entry. I cannot deny being both surprised and pleased at being made an Officer of the Most Excellent Order of the British Empire after just five years in the Service and then a Companion of the Most Distinguished Order of St Michael and St George after twelve years. There are today just 1100 'CMGs' and around forty who hold both CMG and OBE. I must have been doing something well; but it was really Margaret who should have received the decorations. I was just doing my job to the best of my ability; whereas like so many other diplomatic wives Margaret put up with some fairly awful living conditions from time to time.

When people ask me how I became a British Ambassador I reply that it was 'because I married someone who once said she was prepared to go anywhere at any time'. For her contribution to official entertainment and other duties Margaret received no recognition. On the other hand she has probably been kissed by more stars of stage and screen than have most married women: Laurence Olivier, Larry Hagman, Pavarotti, Rolf Harris, Cary Grant and a few others. Margaret may well have felt, at least at the time, that it was worth all the 'packing and following' just to have been kissed by Cary Grant twice on the same day.

My twenty years in Her Majesty's service were a wonderful period, full of worthwhile things to do and so many interesting people to meet. I am very proud to have been able to represent the United Kingdom as a diplomat while Britain was still a force to be counted in international affairs.

Having entered Her Majesty's Diplomatic Service rather late I then managed to negotiate my way out of it a little early. After Hanoi I had just three years to go before I reached the compulsory retiring age of sixty. I was assured that there would be another post, but there was no other Asian post available at the time. I certainly did not want to just fill in three years to my sixtieth birthday as an Ambassador or High Commissioner to a country in which I had no particular interest. There was for me an alternative. I was confident that as a well qualified chartered accountant I should have no trouble finding useful employment in the commercial world for ten years or so. As it turned out, within two months of settling in Double Bay, Sydney, and attracting my first client, I received an offer I could not refuse. We were soon back in London to begin another career that was if anything more international than anything I had done before.

I am fortunate in being able to look back on several careers and to be able to say that I enjoyed them all; though I have no illusions that it would be wise or even agreeable to return to any one of them. Seafaring, accountancy, and even diplomacy are not quite what they were. It is also helpful to look back with some relief to realise that what were occasional disappointments turned out to be blessings in disguise.

My years in merchant ships from the age of sixteen provided me with a base upon which to build later careers. Four years as an apprentice deck officer gave me seven voyages round the world before I was twenty. Those four years were followed by a sea adventure of the 'don't do it again' kind; while for a further three years at sea, I earned a good salary being in effect paid extra to stay on board to study for the next career. It was a great way to spend my youth.

Eight years in the accountancy profession must have included a few dull tasks I suppose. I certainly did a share of 'green ticking' in audits; but public practice taught me a lot about business and businessmen. It even taught me something about criminals. Those years also gave me an opportunity to become involved in local government as an elected member of the Hobart City Council and to test the possibilities for politics generally.

Six years as an Australian Trade Commissioner were good years and with spells in four countries, in addition to time in Canberra, I covered more territory than most did in twice the time. Contrariwise, if in those six years I had not had such an interesting series of posts as a Trade Commissioner, and if terms of employment and prospects for further advancement had been different, I would probably have stayed on.

Twenty years as a member of the British Diplomatic Service could never have been foreseen. My parents and schoolteachers would have been surprised. Those years provided me with the 'encounters of a diplomatic kind', some of which I have related in this memoir.

After diplomacy of the formal kind, five years as the first Chief Executive of the World Coal Institute came about because the big players in the world coal industry decided that their industry needed 'an ambassador with a commercial background' to build an international industry association and to represent the industry at international conferences. The issues of 'global warming' and 'CO_2 emissions' were beginning to gather steam and the environmentalists were blaming much of the problem on coal. Providing a 'Voice for Coal' was a job that brought everything I had done before into play – it even being useful to mention that I had had a coal miner and his wife as foster parents during the war, and had started my working life in a coal-burning ship. WCI also gave me great satisfaction from recruiting a team of young people from five countries, all of whom went on to bigger things after their time working with me in the cause of COAL.

But WCI was not the end. I went on a couple of trade missions to Vietnam and then managed to get elected to Westminster City Council for four years, an activity which didn't produce much by way of income but was worthwhile and produced some interesting experiences. I came to realise that the problems of local government were much the same in the extraordinary City of Westminster as they were in the much smaller but most agreeable City of Hobart: in Westminster the problems were just on a bigger scale.

Then there has been an activity of mine that Margaret has perhaps enjoyed more than any other; and for which she was directly responsible in seeing an opportunity when it appeared before her. As a guest lecturer on cruise ships I may not earn anything at all, but it is a convenient way to revisit places and friends we have both known in my earlier careers. So after sixty years I found myself back where I started – at sea – but in somewhat greater comfort.

Appendices

Telegrams: "MINAG", Nairobi
Telephone: Nairobi 21701-21705

When replying please quote
Ref. No. ...MoA...A.....
            and date

OFFICE OF
THE MINISTER FOR AGRICULTURE
RHODES HOUSE
KENYATTA AVENUE
P.O. Box 30028
NAIROBI, KENYA

...14th..September,........, 19.68

Richard Tallboys, Esq.,
Commonwealth Office,
Downing Street,
London. S.W.1.

Dear Mr Tallboys,

        I am most grateful for the help and advice you
gave to us in London during the week from the 25th
August to 2nd September.

        Colonel Anderson has stressed that he could not
have achieved all he did without the tremendous help
and cooperation which you gave him.

        Very many thanks.

                              yours sincerely,

                              Bruce McKenzie

                        (BRUCE McKENZIE)
                              MINISTER

An unexpected 'thank you' for my help with the contingency planning for President Kenyatta's funeral – a delicate matter since Kenyatta was still alive. Jomo Kenyatta, the best President Kenya has had, went on for another ten years but Bruce Mackenzie died much earlier in a mysterious aircraft crash.

To Col. Wichtrich,
A G A S.

Dear Sir,

In the general rejoicing of the victory of the Allies, victory of democracy & freedom over fascism & oppression - We feel a bit sorry, (1) our American friends are leaving us, (2) we have none or very small share in that democracy & freedom yet.

Anyhow, we will keep on fighting to get our full share. In our first, we remain sure that the sympaty of the great people of America is with us. And when we attain our aim: National independence, We are sure to meet our American friends again, and this, in happier conditions and in larger number.

Lt Phelan is becoming very popular among our guerilles & villagers. Every one of us regret his leaving & hope he could come back here again.

The American pilot downed in DONG TRIEU is safe and sound in the hand of Oversea.Chinese bandits. Our local VML is in pourparler with them. We ordered our local VML to pay whatever sum of money the bandits ask, in order to get the pilot out and to send him back to his HQ.

We thank you very much of sympaty & aid you have given us. We remain sure that in the USA or wherever you be, you will win more friends for our country & our cause

On behalf of VML, I send you a small souvenir - a laque painting by a Tongking artist, member of the VML.

I wish you good health and good luck, and beg to remain

Yours very sincerely.

C. M. Hoo

This letter was written by Ho Chi Minh to US Lt Colonel Wichtrich in 1945 and illustrates how poorly the 'West' understood the motivations of the Vietnamese nationalists. Much tragedy might have been avoided. Reproduced from *MisX*, by A.R. Wichtrich.

MEMORIAL SERVICE

FOR

THE ADMIRAL OF THE FLEET
THE EARL MOUNTBATTEN OF BURMA

SEOUL   SOUTH KOREA   6 SEPTEMBER 1979

Anglican Cathedral, Seoul.

Eulogy written and delivered by
Richard Tallboys
British chargé d'affaires a.i.

BRITISH EMBASSY
SEOUL

That we should remember the life

of

Admiral of the Fleet the Earl Mountbatten
of Burma;

Born on 25 June 1900, himself the younger

son of an Admiral of the Fleet;
Naval cadet at the age of 13
Admiral of the Fleet at the age of 56;

Murdered at the age of 79.

Lord Mountbatten was a man of such an
extraordinarily full and successful life that it
seems an impertinence for an ordinary individual
to stand and speak of him;

Yet the lives of countless millions of
ordinary people have been directly influenced
to some extent or another by his actions and
ideas –

by his example;

by his skill in diplomacy;

and by his ability to lead them, whether he did

so as

Laurence Olivier read a lesson at the memorial service for Earl Mountbatten, without being recognised, but he declined to prepare and deliver the eulogy, so the task fell to me, with the following result. The only comment I received afterwards was 'Did they write that for you in London?'

BRITISH EMBASSY
SEOUL

commander of the naval destroyer

HMS Kelly,

as Supreme Allied Commander in South East
Asia,

as the last Viceroy of India,
or as Chief of Naval Staff.

After a long and full professional naval
career he continued to influence and guide many
men and women, young and old, throughout the
Commonwealth, by his involvement as patron –
president – or ordinary member of a wide range
of community and charitable organisations.

The list of his work is endless; but his
career was not merely one of formal positions and
titles. Whether as naval officer or military
overlord his role was direct and decisive.■
His ideas and leadership in the peaceful transfer
of power in India were crucial to success and to
the lives of millions, generation after generation

But even the finest life can end in senseless

BRITISH EMBASSY
SEOUL

tragedy; not only for a great man such as Lord
Mountbatten but also for those of his family; for
the young boatman, and the 18 ordinary soldiers
who died on the same day.

It is perhaps the saddest commentary of all
on the failure of mankind to follow the teachings
of Christ that Lord Mountbatten
having seen his father's career ended by
prejudice and intolerance
should, 60 years later, have his own life ended
by violence which was itself the product of
prejudice and bigotry just as extreme,
just as incomprehensible, and just as pointless.
WILL WE NEVER LEARN

In his long life Lord Mountbatten successfully reconciled the apparently irreconcilable.
We can but pray that the circumstances of his death –
will lead towards a peace and understanding in
Northern Ireland that has until now
impossible to achieve.

[BY THE PEACE AMONG OUR PEOPLES LET MEN ■
KNOW WE SERVE THE LORD]